The GREATEST
in the WORLD

illustrated by
**Tracy Staskevich**

**Prof Roland Rotherham**

The Greatest
# Etiquette
# & Dining
Tips in the World

A 'The Greatest in the World' book

www.thegreatestintheworld.com

Illustrations:
Tracy Staskevich
www.tracystaskevich.com

Cover & layout design:
the designcouch
www.designcouch.co.uk

Cover images:
© Kathy Burns; © Robert Howarth; © Eric Limon; © Stephen VanHorn
all courtesy of www.fotolia.com

Copy editor:
Bronwyn Robertson
www.theartsva.com

Series creator/editor:
Steve Brookes

Published in 2007 by
The Greatest in the World Ltd., PO Box 3182
Stratford-upon-Avon, Warwickshire CV37 7XW

Text and illustrations copyright © 2007 – The Greatest in the World Ltd.

A CIP catalogue record for this book is available from the British Library
ISBN 978-1-905151-21-9

Printed and bound in China by 1010 Printing International Ltd.

I humbly dedicate this small volume to my parents
who always tried to teach me the importance of
doing things properly and will now know they
have failed dismally.

Also, to my very dear friends
Pat and "Cliff" Clifford,
definitely "the hosts with the most".

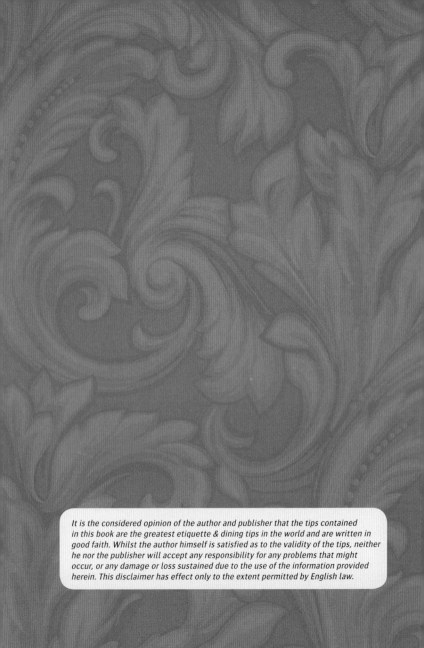

# Contents

# Foreword

Dr Professor Roland Rotherham is, without question, a national treasure ... He is also one of Britain's best-kept secrets. Meet him once – even if it's just for a few moments – and something extraordinary happens. First, you find yourself instantly transfixed by the stunning depth of his knowledge. Next you'll be fully absorbed by his tremendous charm, effortless oratory and boundless enthusiasm. Finally you'll be left intoxicated by his unique humour and refreshing ability to keep his feet firmly fixed to the floor. He's the bloke next door with the most incredible encyclopaedic brain ... pick a subject, any subject – and the Dr will speak!

I first met "Roly" at the BBC's Pebble Mill studios. I was broadcasting my daily radio programme when he arrived for a brief chat on the history of food. Nobody could have prepared me, or the listeners, for what followed. In the next hour, the brief chat turned into a slice of radio magic. Roland instantly captivated both the listeners and me with the remarkable tale of how to stuff a dormouse. Among many other things, he also touched on eating boiled monkey's bottoms in the Himalayan Mountains. Within moments he'd taken us from tussling with vagabonds on top of his trusty camel to being captured by pirates in the jungle – all recalled in mesmerising fashion.

By the end of the show, he'd got the Lady Mayoress of Birmingham impersonating the 1930s singer and actress Jessie Matthews – I'll never forget them both belting out the "Dancing Divinity's" classic song *Over my shoulder goes one care* while scoffing heartily on a batch of Roland's home made mince pies. (Quite simply, Dr Rotherham has that effect on people, and it's a rare talent indeed.) By the time he'd left Pebble Mill, the BBC's switchboard was in meltdown with the whole of the West Midlands wanting to know – and hear – more from "that incredible doctor fellow". The broadcast was eventually entered for – and won – a prestigious Sony Award ... the equivalent of an Oscar in the broadcasting world. Since then, I'm privileged to say, Roland and I have become regular radio sparring partners ... and firm friends.

To be entertained at "Roly Towers" is an unforgettable experience. His ability in the kitchen is legendary and his knowledge of food is incomparable. Furthermore, his kindness and generosity is quite humbling (and his cricket scorebooks are the neatest in the land). While always retaining the common touch, he's a storyteller extraordinaire. He'll have you spellbound, spinning yarn upon yarn on anything and everything from his time in the Royal household to King Arthur and the Holy Grail.  To hear him entertain a crowd remains a thrill ... and now, to have his tales and etiquette & dining tips in print is a sheer delight – I know you'll enjoy reading this book as much as he's enjoyed writing it.

To be asked to pen these few words is truly a great honour.

Malcolm Boyden
BBC Radio Presenter

# et·i·quette

*noun*

1. conventional requirements as to social behavior; proprieties of conduct as established in any class or community or for any occasion.

2. a prescribed or accepted code of usage in matters of ceremony, as at a court or in official or other formal observances.

3. the code of ethical behavior regarding professional practice or action among the members of a profession in their dealings with each other.

# Introduction ...

Dear Reader

This book is written with everyone in mind, whether you are a doyen of dinner parties, a resident 'drone' of the cocktail function, a 'Hyacinth Bucket', or a keen thrower of the soirée with a binge on top. There will, I promise, be something here to make things a little easier for you.

How often have we witnessed the well meaning but all too obvious faux pas? The innocent but recognisable 'clanger' being dropped? It is with sincere hope that you will now be able to avoid the red faced consequences of such actions as we explore the world of entertaining and social graces.

I recall all too well the ill educated bar man, who when asked by me for a glass of rosé gave me a blank and somewhat bemused stare before, to my horror, mixing a glass of red and white wine!

This is your book, and it will cut a sway through the forest of uncertainties and make the correct way open to you. Some of them might seem a little antiquated, that's not the point. This is about 'doing it right' and if it's worth doing, it's worth doing correctly.

Entertain and enjoy but let's do it with style and correctness.

Yours cordially

"Cleanliness and order are not matters of instinct; they are matters of education, and like most great things, you must cultivate a taste for them.

*Benjamin Disraeli*

# The basics

chapter 1

# chapter 1
# The basics

**W**elcome to the world of entertaining, that exciting realm of parties, soirées, functions, and other assorted 'bun fights'. There can possibly be no greater feeling of triumph than knowing you have successfully hosted a party of whatever type and that it has been a success, nay, a great success!

Some people are born hosts/entertainers and find that functions of any kind are easily accomplished; most people however need a little help and advice. Relax dear reader that's what I'm here for. Let's explore the world of entertaining and tackle the potential pitfalls before they occur.

## What's it to be?

First and foremost let us try to ascertain the type of function you might wish to host. They tend to fall into two main categories, those in which you eat too much and those in which you drink too much.

## Keep a clear head

First point, if you are going to be a successful host hold back. By all means let your guests indulge, that's the whole point but you should be careful and try to keep a clear head until the end of the evening. You have guests to look after, and they're your priority.

## Planning is everything

When planning a function of any kind, once you have decided the type of occasion you will host, you will need one very important factor, the guests. Plan carefully who is going to be invited, always make sure guests are compatible.

### Roland's recommendation

**MIX WISELY**

Remember a clash of personalities in your home can be disastrous, this is as important for yourself as for your guests. What could be worse than opening your home to people only to find that (a) one of your guests and yourself have never got on but you have invited them for one reason or another, or (b) that two or more of your guests have a hostility that is being politely veiled by good behaviour for now, remember as the wine flows so do the inhibitions. The last thing you need is to start by hosting a party and end by being the unwilling host of the World Heavyweight Boxing Tournament.

## The invitation

Fine, you have decided who you would like to invite; how do you go about inviting them? The whole area of invitations can be quite murky, let's try to cut through some of the uncertainty.

## Size does matter

How large is your function going to be? Is it going to have, hopefully, more than let us say six guests? The reason we ask questions like this is to ascertain if we need printed invitations.

## Formal or not?

Can we just invite people by telephone? If you are just asking a few friends round for an informal 'nosh' then by all means use your telephone but if you want to make an occasion a little more special then use a written invitation.

## To print or not to print

Pre-printed invitation cards are more than acceptable for the functions you might wish to hold and they are available from many retail stationers. The printed cards have blank areas in which you can fill in the details of the function, the name of the guest or guests and, of course, the details of your address or where the function is destined to be held.

## "Publish and be damned!"

Using a written invitation has two main benefits. It shows you are taking the occasion seriously and it also acts an aide-mémoire to the guests.

## The spurious memory

Nothing is more potentially annoying than going to the trouble of organising a function and having your guests asking "When is it again?" "Where did you say it was?" If you have sent an invitation they have no excuse, the information is at hand.

# *An anecdote*

## Memory can play tricks

Many years ago, more than I care to remember, Her Majesty Queen Elizabeth II was on tour in Australia. One evening a cocktail party had been arranged and many of Australia's noted inhabitants were in attendance.

The party was in full swing and everyone was enjoying a very regal occasion. On the verandah the crystal sparkled in the dying embers of the sun and the warmth of its rays were still noticeable to all who were in attendance.

I feel certain that you have all been in the position whereby you are certain that you recognise someone but are not sure from where?

One of the guests was seen to be staring (not impolitely) at another of the guests, a rather tall gentleman of imposing stature. After a while this perplexed guest gently accosted with a cheery "Good evening", the reply was reciprocated. The first guest asked "How are things?" The reply came "Not bad thanks". Next came "Keeping busy?" "Yes thanks" came the reply. The poor instigator could be seen wracking his brains trying to ascertain from whence he knew the other guest.

After a short pause the expression on his face registered a smile as he believed he had the ideal question to assist him. "Over with the family then?" "Yes" came the reply, "How is the wife?" was asked, "Great thanks" was the reply. "What's she doing these days?" was next thrown across. "Oh you know, still Queen" came the reply from the Duke of Edinburgh!

## Making an impression

If you become a serious host and wish to make your mark in the world of entertaining, you might even wish to have some personalised invitations printed. Again these can allow in their design to have blank areas in which you can fill in the type of function, guests' names etc. Oh go on! It all goes to make it more of a function.

## So to recap

- Choose the type of function you will host.
- Make out your list of who will be invited.
- Decide how you will invite them.
- Mix and match.
- Make a seating plan.
- Prepare well.

"That's the secret of entertaining. You make your guests feel welcome and at home. If you do that honestly, the rest takes care of itself."

*Barbara Hall*

# Dressing
# the room

# chapter 2
# **Dressing the room**

So, we have our guests, we have decided on the type of function, what's left? Of course! We must prepare our home to receive our guests, or as an old friend of mine used to say, "Prepare to repel boarders", although actually you could never wish for a better host.

Let us assume that you have decided initially to host a drinks party, how will we prepare our home for the ensuing hostilities?

## **Preparation is everything**

Firstly address your drawing room/living room; this will be the main theatre for the event and you will want to convey the right ambiance and image.

## Roland's recommendation

### SECURE THE PORCELAIN
Scan your room; does it have any ornaments that are precariously placed and easy to be knocked off their perch? If that is the case move them. Remember this is as much for your guests as for yourself.

## Accidents can happen

If an accident should occur the offending guest will be as mortified as you that one of your precious Crown Derby figurines of the Spice Girls has been toppled, rendering Emma B headless for eternity. Place breakables in view but safely out of elbow range.

## Keep the wood good

Tabletops too should be rendered as damage proof as possible. Drinks mats should be placed at convenient intervals in order that they can be engaged by the base of any offending glass hovering in the vicinity of a polished wooden table.

### Roland's recommendation

**MEET AND GREET**
Always be on hand to welcome your guests personally, no matter what the function. There is no excuse for you not to do this.

## The introduction

When introducing someone always use a clear voice and if introducing someone to your partner mention your partner's name second, like this. "Mrs Alice Thresher, this is my wife Alison" or "Councillor Arnwell, this is my husband Peter Marsh". Do not be afraid to introduce someone as your partner if you are not married, this is perfectly alright and acceptable.

## Offering a libation

Do not offer your guests an empty glass and then proceed to fill it, bad form. The guests should receive an already charged glass from a tray held by you or an assisting friend, relative, or serf.

## And another?

After the initial glass has been proffered and providing that the guest does not change the content of their drink then it is acceptable to refill from a bottle or decanter, unless it involves a mixer such as gin and tonic, then the glass is removed and returned recharged and replenished.

## Beware the drip

When pouring from a bottle into a glass, make sure that you have placed a cloth around the bottle. This reduces the risk of dripping and spillage, particularly if the bottle has been chilled and the body might be moist or even wet from the ice bucket.

## Simplicity itself

The reason behind this is simple; it reduces the risk of spillage when a guest is holding their glass, in particular if they are drinking a mixed drink.

## The born juggler

Don't be afraid to use a serving table. Ask yourself, you are holding a bottle of gin, a bottle of tonic water, a dish of sliced lemon, an ice bucket, are you? How many hands have you got? It makes good serving sense.

# *An anecdote*

## Corrected with a flourish

I well recall some years ago visiting that site of sheer magnificence in Saint James' – Fortnum and Mason. For those of you who do not know this establishment may I suggest that you plan a visit when you are next in Town?

The joy of Fortnums was always the Soda Room; here one can take tea in surroundings of wonderful faded elegance. Whilst entertaining a group of friends the table next to ours was occupied by two American visitors, who quickly made themselves heard above the other guests.

With a snap of the fingers (oh dear!) they summoned the gentleman who was the head floor walker of the room. A resplendent and regal gentleman of my acquaintance who ruled the room with great authority.

As he approached them the man who had clicked his fingers asked 'Bring us two glasses of iced tea and make sure mine's a clean glass'. Those of us who knew the situation were curious as to the outcome of this request but the Domo merely smiled and bowed and things got back to normal.

After a moment our old friend returned with a chilled jug of iced tea that looked very inviting. It stood on a polished salver with two crystal goblets and folded by them was a spotless white napkin. The Doyen then placed the salver on the table and raised one of the glasses; he inspected it and then polished it with the napkin he had brought. He inspected it yet again and indeed polished it again. Satisfied with its appearance he then asked the two occupants of the table 'Now gentlemen, whose was the clean glass?'

I now know the meaning of 'deafening silence'!

# Going green

Why not use natural greenery from your garden or a good florist to decorate your table and the room? Strands of foliage when laid onto a table can look stunning between each place setting. You can use greenery to decorate shelves and staircases as well. If you have your own garden this is easily achieved and the effect can be stunning.

# Tie a yellow ribbon

Or any other colour that you feel will complement the foliage. You can make garlands this way and your guests will be pleased with the effect and you will have the knowledge that 'It's all my own work'!

# That Yuletide touch

Evergreens, such as ivy and fir are superb for Christmas decoration. Tie these with red ribbon and the effect is sumptuous. Using these between place settings is most effective.

Just take care you wash your greenery first, we don't want any unwanted little visitors travelling over the table during courses.

# The glittering occasion

Be warned, it has become very popular of late to sprinkle your table with small sequins and glitter for festive occasions. These can be atrocious, they scatter and fall and can make the most awful mess. No matter how careful you are in cleaning up you can find that these little rascals can reappear for months if you are not extra vigilant.

## Let's look at what we have done so far

- Make sure that all of the rooms to be used are spotless; clean and polish like your life depended on it. Your reputation does.

- Remove all valuables in case of damage. Either place them in accessible places or remove them altogether.

- Make sure that your polished wood surfaces are protected. (Cloths or drinks mats).

- Wrap bottles in clean white cloths whilst pouring, especially if using a chilled wine.

- Make sure all glasses and allied items contain no tell tale smudges.

- You may decorate using floral arrangements if you wish.

- Try using greenery with ribbons to add more colour.

- Avoid 'sprinkles'!

# Ask the professor...

**Q** *When should a gentleman remove his hat?*

**A** A gentleman should always remove his hat when entering a home, restaurant, theatre, or church. And of course, whenever meeting a lady or a member of nobility.

**Q** *When a man calls off a wedding should a woman give the engagement ring back?*

**A** Yes it is only correct and proper that the lady return the unwanted ring.

**Q** *How should one sneeze or cough in public?*

**A** If you feel a sneeze or cough coming, cover your nose or mouth with your left hand if you are right handed, whilst holding your handkerchief in you left hand. This leaves your right hand free and clean for action such as opening doors.

After all, what is
your host's purpose
in having a party?
Surely not for you
to enjoy yourself;
if that were their sole
purpose, they'd have
simply sent champagne
and women over to
your place by taxi.

*P.J. O'Rourke*

# The drinks party

# chapter 3
# **The drinks party**

**A**h, so, the drinks party is on the list is it? Very well let us see how we can accomplish the very epitome of the drinks party, indeed a party that will forever carve your name in the hall of fame as the host with the most.

## Make your choice

As we have done with the guest list and choosing our function, we must now tackle the same question. What type of party is it to be? If you have decided to host a drinks party, whether it is of the cocktail variety or something less formal in the genre, never lay on too much variance in drinks.

## K.I.S.S.

'Keep It Simple, Stupid!' As with dressing 'less is more'. If you wish to serve a beer allow one to two types of a better beer. If serving wine then one type of white and one of red will be more than sufficient.

## Shorts?

You can augment your bar with a single malt whisky or even a gin if you wish.

## The designated driver

Always remember the driver. Make a jug of iced tea or fruit juice.

# How long should it last?

Something to bear in mind is the duration of your party, in other words, how long do you want it to last?

## Roland's recommendation

**SHORT AND SWEET**

An old friend of mine once had the idea of placing bottles of vodka and schnapps in his deep freeze. He issued each person with a small shot glass and proceeded to fill them up with amazing speed, having no need for ice. Needless to say, not a party of long duration but one of great effect.

## Kick off

Also, when sending invitations state a time for arrival, and a time for departure if you wish. This must be handled with delicacy but one of the most diplomatic ways is to state: "Reception at 8 pm. Carriages at 12 midnight". The use of the term 'carriages' will make many smile but the message will be clear. If you have friends you want to stay longer merely ask them to hang back, or even offer them an overnight stay.

## State your times

If you are hosting a function during the day again state the times you wish. You may say 'Between 2 and 7pm'. This is similar to the 'Open House' or 'At Home', so popular in years gone by. However when sending out your invitations to a day event do not write it too pompously.

## Best left unsaid

I am reminded of a certain 'Lady C' who sent out invitations, one being sent to George Bernard Shaw, stating 'Lady C will be at home between 2 and 6 pm on the 12th of May, R.S.V.P.' only to receive the reply from George Bernard Shaw 'So will George Bernard Shaw'.

# The cheese and wine party

How very civilised. What could be nicer, a glass of wine, good company and a nice selection of cheeses. There are pitfalls to avoid however ...

## Serving wine

Stick to one basic red and one white. A rosé is fine by way of a change if you wish. As a general rule of thumb, red wine tends to be served at room temperature, whilst white wine is served, again generally, slightly chilled. This is however, all down to personal taste. I know of some red wines that are fine when served a little on the cool side and, indeed, there are some white wines that benefit from not being too chilled.

## Rosé is rosy

Rosé is in a field by itself, here you have a superbly light and crisp wine that is incredibly versatile and which you can serve either at room temperature or, indeed, slightly chilled. However beware over chilling. Why? Well this will only detract from its flavour rendering it dull and lifeless.

# Le fromage!

Choose no more than about five types of cheese. Any more is unnecessary and will only confuse. Try serving a blue cheese, a good Cheddar, a smoked cheese, a cream cheese, (I like goats – super!), and perhaps a speciality, herb infused offering. Please try to avoid those of an anti-social nature. Not everyone will appreciate your Carpathian non-sterilised roulé with extra garlic and a chilli crust.

# Beer is fine

If you have decided to serve beer, as we discussed earlier, only one or two types are necessary. I suggest, and here I am assuming that as you will be serving beer the function will be slightly less formal than normal, choose a light lager type and a darker bitter type.

## Keeping it well

Make sure your beers are chilled but beware, placing bottles in the deep freeze will certainly chill them quickly, but can also cause bottle led eruptions that will result in the beers virtually exploding in the freezer. Very messy and awful to clear up.

## What to choose?

There are many to choose from. Europe produces first rate bottled beer and it is bottles I would recommend for this type of gathering. A German or Dutch lager or light beer, perhaps of the 'palm' type and then a darker type, perhaps a 'Bok' beer, very tasty but be warned, they can come with a kick. Many of Europe's beers have a higher specific gravity than those from England.

# Serving champagne

Champagne is one of the great classics of any drinks party. However, opening the bottle causes some people unnecessary distress. The rules are simple, once you have removed the foil and wire that hold the cork in place you grasp the cork firmly and whilst holding it steady you turn the bottle. Never, ever, turn and pull the cork from the bottle.

## What about the temperature?

Champagne should be served at a temperature of around 45°. This is the optimum to get the best out of the flavour of this delicious, if expensive, drink.

## By the sword

One spectacular method is to open the bottle using a sword; but beware, this is only for the brave, not to be tried by the faint hearted, spectacular though it might look. There is a weakness specially built in to the champagne bottle just below the cork that allows the neck to be sheared off cleanly by a blade that resembles that of a sword.

## What about the glasses?

Many people these days use the tulip or flute shaped glasses. I can see the attraction as their shape is graduated, they do tend to hold the effervescence of the champagne more than the old saucer style glasses. However, I still cling to the saucer shaped glasses, I find comfort in the feel of the bowl resting in my fingers. The choice is up to you.

### Roland's recommendation

**POURING IT**

When pouring champagne, please remember you are not handling a bottle of beer. Initially pour no more than 1 inch into each glass, allowing it to settle. You may then continue to fill the glass but to no more than two thirds full. Hold the glass gently but firmly by the stem, try to avoid using the bowl, which also means the warmth of your hand will not interfere with the temperature of the chilled champagne.

## Champagne cocktails

One of my favourites is the pink champagne cocktail. This could not be easier to make. Using a champagne glass of your choice place in the glass a cube of sugar, drip onto this a few drops of Angostura bitters. Next pour into the glass a measure of brandy, then top up with the champagne of your choice. Delicious and dangerous. What more could you ask?

## Frosting the glass

This is always a treat when serving cocktails and it couldn't be simpler. Just wipe around the rim of the glass with a piece of lemon or lime, then dip the rim of the glass into caster sugar. It looks theatrical and is ideal for that special occasion.

## Meet and greet

Always remember to be ready to greet your guests as they arrive and have a glass of something ready for them. Your guests are your prime concern and their comfort is your sole charge. I know I've said this before but it's of great importance and deserves reiteration.

## Hire in glasses?

If your party guests are old friends and not too many in number, say six or eight of them, then certainly use your own glasses. However, if you are anticipating more than a dozen or so by all means hire your glasses. There is nothing wrong with this and your local kitchen shop or supermarket might well have the contact details of your local catering hire firm, they may even provide the service themselves.

## Hire in crockery?

The same applies to large quantities of plates and cutlery (twelve or more); it will remove some of the stress from yourself and breakages will no longer be a prime concern. The local telephone directory will also contain the details of local catering hire companies as will the Internet.

## Pack it away

Remember if your Stewart Crystal goblets are trampled on by Uncle Igor reliving his exploits whilst on holiday in Greece, your thoughts may turn to homicide; if the latter threat is removed then your crystal is safe to play another day.

## Self service

You might decide to house a free for all. You know the sort of thing, an assortment of drinks and an eclectic mix of people. My advice is to set up a bar station – a place where all the drinks are available.

### Roland's recommendation

**HELPING OUT**

It would also be good idea to ask a family member or a friend to assist in order that the bar station is still mainly used by yourself and the drinks are still served to your guests. This way you still show yourself as a good host.

# Waste not, want not!

Most importantly, you also avoid the phenomena of everyone congregating in the kitchen area and, as if things could not get worse, opening the bottles themselves. This can leave you afterwards with a plethora of half empty, or half full, bottles of varying and dubious quality necessitating pouring the contents away whilst bewailing the waste.

# The essential nibbles

Even though you are ostensibly hosting a 'drinks party' please bear in mind that you will need food for your guests, I look on it as 'blotting paper'. You might actually be surprised at the number of times I have been invited to a drinks party to find that it was purely that – 'drinks' – and not a solid in sight.

## What to use

There is no need at all to go overboard. Even the simplest of food will be more than adequate for a simple drinks function. Again, rather than having guests again attempting to help themselves, this is an area you can pre-prepare and have waiting on serving dishes and trays to pass around as the evening develops.

## Biscuits are good

Using the array of savoury biscuits available and a variety of pâtés and cheeses you can create a simple but perfectly acceptable accompaniment to any function.

# Pre-theatre refreshments

One of my favourites is certainly 'pre-theatre refreshments'. This is a short but delightful party held prior to you all going on to the theatre or ballet, or indeed some other evening function. The layout and conduct could not be simpler …

## Elegance itself

Prior to your friends arriving make sure you have your white wine chilled in the fridge. For this function it is not normal to serve red as it does not complement the rest of the small table. Have the following ready on your serving dishes: asparagus tips rolled in small squares of buttered brown bread, similar with smoked salmon and, if you wish, a small quantity of lightly scrambled egg. You may then change into black tie and get ready to greet your guests. This light, early supper is perfect prior to 'going on' and it sets off the mood for the evening beautifully. Elegant and very enjoyable.

## Chapter summary

- Select your drinks with care.

- The most expensive is not always the best!

- Don't go overboard.

- Keep the selection simple, do not be over complicated.

- Hire in glasses if you wish; your local 'Cook Shop' will help you.

- State the time for 'Kick off'.

- Make sure everyone knows what time 'carriages' are booked for.

- Choose self-service or assisted.

- Select food carefully. Avoid the anti-social.

- Keep an eye on half used bottles, take over the service to avoid waste.

- Don't forget the driver.

Etiquette means
behaving yourself
a little better than
is absolutely essential.

*Will Cuppy*

# The table

chapter 4

# chapter 4
# **The table**

When preparing for a function nothing is as important as your table. This is the stage on which your success will stand, or (unthinkably) fail. Remember, as with the food, people eat with their eyes.

## **What is the function?**

Once again it is your choice of function, what is it to be? Dinner, lunch, or maybe even breakfast? A breakfast party can be great fun and is ideal for those of you who might be slightly put off by catering for a full dinner engagement.

## **Breakfast then!**

Very well, that's settled, we shall look at breakfast as your function and work on from there.

## **The breakfast table**

This is a simple table and one that is easily achieved properly. First remember that a breakfast table uses a cloth. Plain white is the best. Match this with plain white napkins.

## **The silver?**

Again, simplicity itself. All you will require for each place setting is 1 table fork, 1 table knife, 1 dessert spoon and, perhaps, 1 butter knife of the individual type.

## Arranging

Each place setting should be laid with the table fork on the left of the plate and the table knife on the right, the dessert spoon should also be on the right and outside the knife. This is to be used for your first course (cereal, fruit, etc) with the knife and fork for the cooked "main" course.

## The butter knife?

This is to go on the left hand side and at right angles over the side plate; if you do not have butter knives please don't worry, you can easily use dessert knives, but place these at an angle of 45° on the side plate itself.

## What to serve?

If you are inviting guests round for breakfast why not treat them to something a little special?

## May I suggest a kedgeree?

A luxurious and simple dish of rice with chopped hard-boiled eggs and smoked haddock. A touch of elegance and a hark back to Edwardian splendour.

### Roland's recommendation

**WHAT ABOUT TOAST?**

Toast is perfect as are croissants. When eating them however do not cut and butter but tear them up and place your butter onto the plate, butter from there.

*The breakfast table*

## Marmalade or jam?

BOTH! There you go.

## Tea and coffee

Serve a fresh coffee, in a pot, of course, and the same with tea.
The coffee should not be too strong, the tea should.

## Types of tea

For breakfast may I suggest a Darjeeling or Ceylon, most
refreshing and ideal for this time of day. Please though, use
leaf tea and not bags!

## Roland's recommendation

**DOING THE "CONTINENTAL"**

Ah, shades of 'Fred and Ginger'! If you choose a lighter repast try providing a continental alternative. Sliced cheeses, Gouda, Leerdammer etc and sliced cold meats like ham or varied salamis. These can be accompanied with hard-boiled eggs and fruit.

## One stage further

Perhaps you might like to serve Devilled Kidneys, how luxurious is that? Serve them on toast and finish off with a single glass of claret. Only one! You don't want your guests 'swaying but courtly' after breakfast.

## The timing

Timing is important. If you are inviting friends round then suggest a time of 10am which is perfect for a relaxing meal. If they are staying overnight, a little earlier, perhaps 9am?

# Lunch

Lunch is that meal generally consumed at mid-day. Please, always 'lunch' and never 'dinner'. Arrgh!

## The covering

The lunch table resembles the breakfast equivalent somewhat as it too is covered with a cloth, although this can be lightly coloured if you wish. Again napkins should match.

## Flowers?

Certainly if you wish. They should be light and unobtrusive. Informal yet elegant.

## How many courses?

Generally speaking limit yourself to three for lunch. A first course and then main. You may then supply a pudding if you wish, or cheese. Or you may serve both, making four courses in all, depending on the occasion.

## The silver placing?

Again try to keep it simple, this is lunch not dinner. If you are serving soup first then you will require a soup spoon and a butter knife for the attendant bread rolls. The main course will need a table knife and fork and the pudding a dessertspoon and fork. Cheese will only need a dessert knife.

## Good old "Goddards"

Are you using silver or silver plated cutlery and dishes? Take care that they are properly polished. When removing the polish from inaccessible places such as decorated areas or fork prongs, try using a soft toothbrush.

## More bubbles

This time it's soap. If you have used silver polish on items that will be used for food please remember that they must be washed. I once attended dinner where this was not done properly and the colonic effects were devastating and of biblical proportions.

## What if you are not serving soup?

Choose a light first course well. If you choose a pâté and toast for example you will only need an extra dessert knife. Think and plan, all will be well.

## The style?

Use something simple for lunch. Choose the one you are comfortable with.

## Making a placing

Looking at the table setting for each person you should lay up as follows. The table knife and fork should be placed next to the plate. The soup spoon should then go on the outside of the knife, the butter knife is then placed at right angles over the attending side plate. The dessert spoon and fork should go at the top of the place setting facing left to right.

## Messy fingers

For lunch fold your napkins simply, nothing extravagant is needed. Place the folded napkin on the side plate.

## Booze!

That got your attention. Choose your glasses to complement what you are serving. A simple wine glass is fine, and next to it place a water glass. Not everyone will consume vast quantities of 'Red Biddy' at lunch and many will want water.

*The lunch table*

## What to serve?

Try not to produce wines that are too heavy. White or red should be refreshing. Please remember that some of your guests might have to go on to work afterwards. Or at least engage is some activity post lunch.

### Roland's recommendation

**WHAT ABOUT PORT?**
Alright, go on then. If it is a long and relaxing meal then by all means go the whole hog. Serve cheese and the attendant port. Always very pleasant.

## Coffee

For lunch you should serve coffee at the table, as it gives you a chance to talk while still relaxed.

### Roland's recommendation

**WHAT ABOUT THE TIME?**
For lunch I would suggest a time of around 12:30pm for guests to arrive and be seated for 1pm.

## Pre-lunch drinks?

Certainly. Why not go with the good old 'G&T'? It's what made Britain great and gave it a slightly dodgy liver! If you want to play safe then serve sherry, drier is good.

## Courses on the table?

Certainly, this is quite acceptable. However, if you do have a side-serving table then feel free to place your courses on it and allow guests to help themselves.

## How long for lunch?

This is up to you. I have been to some lunch parties that started at 12:30 and I have arrived back at my home well into the evening. It's your call.

## The softness of majesty

On one particular and very memorable occasion Her Majesty Queen Elizabeth the Queen Mother had invited a number of Her personal household to lunch. Please remember that Her Majesty's officers were indeed all gentlemen "of a certain age" and lunch was long and glorious.

The day could not have been more pleasant, the warm sun shining and the birds singing as only they could when doing so for this remarkable lady. After they had finished eating Her Majesty suggested that perhaps they might like to take drinks out in the garden of Clarence House and so they all duly decamped to the garden where sitting in the warm sun and drinking softly of Her Majesty's excellent wines the day overwhelmed them.

One by one these aged and elegant gentlemen, accompanied by Her Majesty, slowly drifted off into the arms of Morpheus. The garden was filled with the sounds of the warm summer breeze gently ruffling the plumage of the shrubs and the even softer sounds of this great lady and her officers gently sleeping away the afternoon.

Even her personal equerry was overcome and, when he awakened, realised the horror of all these people falling asleep in Her Majesty's presence; simply not done.

Waking Her gently, she proceeded to talk as if nothing had happened as one by one her gentlemen stirred, back into the afternoon air and the company of this gracious lady.

## Alfresco?

Most certainly. If the weather permits and you have a garden suitable why not! Please be warned though, if your residence is situated on the M6 this is not a good idea, similarly if your house is under the main flight path of Heathrow, eat inside!

## Is the table the same?

Yes, in every way. Though if you are eating outside make sure that you prepare well in advance and also be prepared for a change in the weather. Nibbling daintily and retaining one's poise is not really possible in a force 9 gale.

# Tea time

Once again you have choices to make. A standard tea or that dying but magnificent alternative 'High Tea'. Let's look at the standard tea first. For this function a full table is not always necessary. You may use the table to contain all the food and allow people to serve themselves and sit around your drawing/living room if you wish. However if you wish to sit at table then follow these simple rules.

## Setting the table

The table should, again, be cloth covered. Each place must have one plate of suitable size; (a standard dessert plate is usually sufficient). Each guest must also have a dessert knife. A small tea-napkin is also essential. These are much smaller than the lunch or dinner variety and can be coloured and embroidered if you wish.

*The standard tea table*

## The essential cups

The tea cup is a thing of beauty. Choose your china carefully.
It should be fine but usable. The handle of the cup and the
spoon should both point to 'half past four' on the saucer.
After all, it is tea time!

## Holding the cup properly

When holding the teacup, or coffee cup, merely grasp
the handle gently but securely with the pads of your thumb
and index finger. This is more than enough to secure the cup
for the purpose of drinking.

## Lose the digit

Please, never raise your small finger whilst drinking. This is deplorable and should be rewarded by the offending digit being immediately removed by a pair of hot sugar tongs. Serves you right too!

## Stirring the cup

If you take sugar, you will therefore need to stir your tea or coffee. This should be done silently and never, ever, with the profane tinkling of the spoon striking the sides of the cup.

## Pastry forks?

If you wish, yes. If you do not possess these items then a dessert fork is acceptable. Perhaps I might politely suggest the purchase of some pastry forks should you wish to have such occasions often?

## The napkin

Once again a simple fold is all that is necessary. Place it gracefully onto the plate.

## Making the tea at the table

This is a great joy. If you have a spirit kettle it is simplicity itself. If you have to use an electric kettle then by all means make your tea in the kitchen and bring it through.

## Bags or leaf?

Always leaf, without question. Tea bags have no place at a formal tea party. Good quality tea is essential. Try serving two varieties. A green China tea and perhaps an Indian alternative. Don't forget the quintessentially English Earl Grey.

## A strain but worth it

Use a good tea strainer. Some very attractive models are available. If you can get one to match your cutlery all the better.

## Roland's recommendation

**HOW TO POUR**

Never put the strainer onto the cup. Hold it above and then, with the other hand gently pour. Please, never shake the pot to deliver off the last drops. That would not even happen in a Lyons Corner House let alone your drawing room. (Whatever happened to the Corner Houses?)

## M.I.F. Oh no!

Milk in first? Most certainly not! Pour the tea first and then ask if your guest wants milk, add a little, no more. Also, keep a well-sliced lemon on hand for those who might like the alternative.

## Is it science?

Yes, if you pour the milk into the cup first and then add the tea you will scald the milk. This does subtly change the flavour.

## Sweets for the sweet

Sugar lumps are still popular for formal teas. Use tongs, the sight of grubby digits ferreting around in the sugar bowl is not conducive to an elegant occasion.

## The food

Choose your food for tea with care. A variety of sandwiches is good. Three or four types will be excellent. The ubiquitous cucumber, smoked ham or tongue, egg salad with anchovy, and perhaps a subtle cheese are perfect.

## The cake

Cake is, of course, a must for tea. Serve at least two types of cut cake and two types of individual pastry. A good fruit cake is marvellous as is something of a rather richer creamy variety. Try éclairs or buns of some type. Very traditional and very tasty.

# The high tea

This is a totally different animal. For high tea one should sit at table at all times. This is more of a formal occasion.

## The high tea table

The table should hold the same as a normal a tea but should include a table knife and fork for each guest.

## Plating it up

The main plate for High Tea should be of a larger size than a normal dessert plate. You are serving more substantial and, indeed, hot food.

*The high tea table*

## Roland's recommendation

**WHAT TO SERVE?**

Allow me to suggest some good old favourites. I would consider kippers, a good source of flavour and superb for this type of table. Again the devilled kidneys will always be a treat. Start with your main dish and then proceed to the sandwiches, (if necessary) but then certainly serve your cakes. This type of tea is far more substantial and ideal if dinner is to be late or children are eating with you.

# The dinner table

This is your ultimate venture. This table more than any other will take your time and all your skill. Please remember, your dinner table has no cloth, it should polished wood.

## The silverware

As with any occasion choose your style of cutlery well and with care. Some amongst you will consider using a modern, contemporary design and others amongst you the more traditional designs. Either way follow these next steps to balance your table well.

## Roland's recommendation

**SPACING IT OUT**
When placing your silverware on the table, always pay attention to the comfort of your guests. There should be enough room for each knife, fork or spoon for each course whilst at the same time ensuring your guests do not end up in arm-locked combat whilst trying to eat.

## Where to put the food

Placing the food on the table is an exact science. When laying your table have a 'dry run' with your empty serving dishes before committing yourself.

## On the mat

Do you want to use a place mat? It can be advisable as it protects your table from the heat of the plates which can leave marks on its surface. You can purchase some very attractive types. I myself, have some that contain a picture of Roly Towers, quite splendid, really!

## The laying of the cutlery

Choose how many courses you are serving. Normally four is acceptable, five is excellent and six or more is absolutely 'tsarist' in decadence.

Lay your cutlery out as in previous meals, working from the outside for your first course and thence inwards to your main and subsequent dishes.

With a formal dinner party, if you are serving a pudding the dessertspoon and fork take their place alongside the other utensils and are not placed over the setting as in lunch.

*The dinner table*

chapter 4

## Old design cutlery?

You might be fortunate to own old silverware. If this is the case and the style is similar to the traditional 'Rat Tail' or 'Fiddle, Thread and Shell', then you may turn your spoons and forks over in order that the base design is shown along with its attendant hallmarks. Please remember this is only acceptable with these styles and then only if your items are over 200 years old.

## How many courses?

As I mentioned earlier, this is up to you. Don't over stretch yourself. Remember you have to cook it. If you are serving soup then you will require soup spoons, don't forget the butter knife with this. Actually in Victorian times the soup was served and a tablespoon was used to eat it.

## Fishy business

You might wish to serve fish after soup and if this the case you may use 'fish eaters'; if you do not have them fear not, the Victorians used two table forks to tease apart the fish and eat with. Go on, turn the clock back!

## The main course

If you have served a fish course, do not repeat it with a fish main course. Use imagination. Meat should be carved at the table by the head of the household. If you are using individual meat servings, (the ubiquitous chop), then you may serve these directly to each guest as the plates are put down. If you are serving game allow one small bird per person or if the bird is larger, pheasant for example, allow half a bird.

## Pudding

Ah, my favourite course. A dessertspoon and fork here are the next items in.

## Savoury?

You might wish to serve a savoury course, something like 'Devils on Horseback', for which you will need a dessert fork and knife.

## Don't forget the cheese

For this course you will need a dessert knife and the butter knife in its normal position by the side plate, this plate should be fresh for the cheese course. Use individual butters, it makes a nice change.

### Roland's recommendation

**EATING OFF YOUR KNIFE!**
Yes, absolutely. When eating cheese at the table it is very good manners to bite the biscuit and then take your cheese delicately from the blade of the knife with your mouth. Don't let anyone tell you different.

## Dessert

Aha, now I have caught you out! You thought we had already covered it with pudding did you not? Go on admit it. Dessert is served separately at the end of the meal and consists of fresh fruit.

## Roland's recommendation

**THE DESSERT SERVICE**

Now for something unusual, your dessert service and its attendant spoons/forks and knives need not match your previous service. Indeed, in days past the dessert service was the diamond in the crown of the dinner table. More elaborate than most it boasted elegance, style, and colour. Minton and Worcester produced most memorable services.

## Having a dibble!

The finger bowl is important for dessert services. This should be of good quality cut-glass or crystal and be half filled with plain or scented water. The bowl is normally placed in front of the diner on a dessert plate with a small napkin under it. This elegant piece of dinner usage has all but died out I fear except in the most prestigious of households.

If you ever have dinner in the mess of a Royal Naval establishment or, indeed, some military gatherings of a similar status you will find a most intriguing thing takes place after dessert is served and before the serving of the port for the 'Loyal Toast'.

As dessert finishes and the glass is filled for the 'Toast' the finger bowl is removed from the table. This dates back to the 18th century when the toast was, of course, 'Gentlemen, The King'. After the Jacobite Rebellion that ended in 1745 after the bloody battle of Culloden and resulted in Prince Charles Edward Stewart fleeing the country, there were ...

... a number of Jacobite sympathisers in the armed forces. As the toast was given it was found that some officers were to be seen saying 'The King' whilst passing their glasses very subtly over the finger bowls, thus toasting "The King Over The Water" – Prince Charles Edward Stewart. Consequently, there should be no finger bowl for the Loyal Toast.

Another interesting point of etiquette, again with regard to the Royal Navy at dinner time, is that the "Loyal Toast" is always given whilst seated. This dates back to the time when the messes on board the sailing ships had very low and heavily beamed ceilings, you remained seated in order that you did not brain yourself on the beams. This tradition remains today.

## Silver gilt!

Now, there's posh! Your dessert cutlery may be of silver gilt if you wish but remember, you must clear the table of all other items before serving it, except the glasses for dessert of course.

### Roland's recommendation

**THE FLORAL DECORATION**
The table centre is traditionally decorated with a floral arrangement, however there is one thing to bear in mind. The size of the arrangement should be impressive but not obtrusive. You do not want your guests being issued with Kukris in order to hack their way to the table or to see each other.

## The napkin

The dinner gives you the opportunity to show off, use it!
Your napkins can now be folded to make elegant shapes to
decorate your place settings. If the origami of this eludes you
don't panic. If you wish no-one will mind if you use a napkin
ring of the silver variety. They hold the napkin in place and
can look very decorative. Infinitely better than being presented
with a piece of limp cloth resembling a diseased giraffe.

## The cruet

If you wish to serve salt, pepper, and mustard then please
invest in a decent cruet set. Very reasonably silver plated
varieties are available.

## The crystalware

Good glass is the essence. If you are serving four courses you
will need four glasses. Let us say a tall 'Hock' glass for fish,
a more substantial 'Claret' glass for your main course, perhaps
a smaller glass for 'Dessert' wine and finally a 'Port' glass.
Arrange them in a clockwise fashion.

Allow me to congratulate you. You are now primed and ready.

## Just to recap then

- Does your table need a cloth? Remember, for dinner it is polished wood.
- Is your table big enough? Do you want to use a console table for serving?
- Check that your napkins match your table cloth, this does not apply to a dinner table.
- If you cannot master folding then just place simply after being freshly ironed.
- Use a place mat if possible. This reduces the risk of heat marks on the table.
- If you are using silver or silver plate cutlery, make sure that you wash it well before use.
- Check your glasses are all clean and place them in order at each setting.
- If you are using floral decoration make sure it's not too big.
- Prepare well in advance. Are your serving dishes ready?
- Plan your courses. Can you cope with what you have chosen to serve?
- When pouring tea, pour the milk in last. Don't rest the strainer on the cup.
- Plan your sandwiches and cakes in advance.
- Double-check your requirements for the table for every function you plan.

- Make sure your guests are aware of timings for your function.
- Place your cruet set, if you use one, in easy reach of your guests.
- Do not clutter your table, don't be afraid of plating up elsewhere.
- Check and check again! Be sure that all is in preparation.
- Never be afraid to obtain help. Better to get assistance than fail.

A dinner invitation,
once accepted, is
a sacred obligation.
If you die before
the dinner takes
place, your executor
must attend.

*Ward McAllister*

# The dinner party

# chapter 5
# The dinner party

Ah, dear reader, the minefield of the dinner party. Not really, trust me – it's a doddle. As with any function choose your menu and choose your guests. I'm sorry to sound repetitive but these are important issues.

## Roland's recommendation

**ARE THERE ANY VEGETARIANS COMING?**
If any of your guests are either vegetarian or vegan please try to cater accordingly. Nothing depresses the poor dears so much as being confronted by slabs of still twitching beef with the blood oozing over the plate. They go quite pale!

## Invite a rogue!

We all know one. Someone who can get away with telling a risqué joke and liven up the proceedings. A good rogue can be worth their weight in caviar.

## If you are a guest

Please bear in mind that a little naughtiness is super but most people do not find Roy "Chubby" Brown appealing at all. Be warned.

## Timing

Most important, timing can be essential for a good dinner party. May I suggest arrival at 7:30pm in order to eat at 8pm? This is perfect for most hosts and guests alike. One tip though, if you are cooking rice do not put it on until everyone has arrived, no-one likes glutinous rice and the outcome is perhaps better employed sealing that rather loose slate on your garage roof.

## Your duty as a guest

Be on time. Early is fine but not too early. I would say 15 minutes at the most, the last thing your host wants is to be seen in their curlers or applying their surgical abdominal support prior to the commencing of hostilities.

## Should I take wine?

Try not to take wine for that evening. Your host will already have organised it. By all means take champagne, always acceptable, or even a good Port for later.

### Roland's recommendation

**WHAT CAN I TAKE?**

Why not offer to supply the coffee? Make it something special. Or how about after-dinner chocolates of the truffle variety? Super. Certainly flowers if you wish, they are always welcomed into a house and make such a nice gesture.

## How to serve

Again, you have choices open to you. You can arrange for the food to placed on the table or plated in the kitchen. You might even try the console table I mentioned earlier but how about having a word with your friendly local restaurant and seeing if one of the waiters has an evening off and will be willing to wait on table for you? Super! You have now impressed everyone.

## Roland's recommendation

**DRINKS FIRST**

You may offer a choice of course but why not try a cocktail? I still love that old favourite the "Gin and It"! Here is my recipe, it could not be simpler.

Use goblet glasses and wipe each rim with a lime. Dip the rim then into caster sugar. Fill each glass with crushed ice and add a generous slug of gin. Top up with Italian vermouth of the "Rosso" type and finish off with a twist of lime. Oh my word yes! This is the cocktail of heroes.

## Even more nibbles

Serve a little something to your guests to accompany the pre-dinner drinks. Small canapés will be perfect but keep them simple. Don't detract from your hard work in the kitchen with the main meal.

## Who sits where?

Why not make out a small seating plan? Using cards and a small covered tray you can arrange your guests accordingly and they can see at a glance where they are to be seated. If they are all old friends, why not make a seating plan using small cartoons or nicknames, it all adds to conviviality.

## Bring it on!

Once all your guests are seated you can start the meal itself. If you are using a waiter for the night please make sure that each dish is offered to your guests to their left and that the guest can help themselves from the proffered dish with the necessary serving spoon and fork.

## Take it off

When clearing dishes they should always be removed from the right of the guest.

## Don't hog it

Even if your favourite food is being served take no more than your share. Gluttony is not seen as a social skill.

## A nasty taste?

If, heaven forefend, you are served something that you believe will either disagree with you or an item that you are aware you should not eat (due to an allergy, etc) diplomatically tell your host. Don't tell lies. You might be invited again and receive the same dish!

# *An anecdote*

## The moveable feast

During one particular dinner party of some notoriety the unknowing waiting footman provided the guests with an amusement that would linger in the minds of many.

Two of the more glittering guests were a certain Lord and Lady who had been seated almost opposite one another. The dinner was proceeding perfectly. The drinks had been superbly mixed, dispensed, and demolished and the first course had been magnificent.

The main course was brought in and found to be pheasant, perfection. Then in the gentle flickering of the candles the staff came round the table and offered the vegetables to each person seated.

Amongst the dishes was a particularly inviting dish of 'sugar snap peas', delicately buttered and steaming in the silver dish.

As the dish was proffered to His Lordship, Her Ladyship was heard to trumpet, "No peas for His Lordship. They make him unfortunate"!

# An anecdote

## An Englishman abroad

Very recently I had the good fortune to visit my surviving family in Germany, in fact it was the occasion of my dear father's 80th birthday. As well as guests from the locale I brought over two very dear friends of my own to join the festivities.

Owing to restricted accommodation my friends had booked into a very pleasant and locally based 'Bed and Breakfast' facility of particularly high standards. When breakfast arrived on the morning of their first day's stay, as you can imagine, the table was well laid and contained a plethora of cold meats, cheeses, breads, jams, scrambled eggs and sausages, together with lashings of fresh coffee. My friends did the 'British' thing and valiantly consumed all on the table.

They spoke of the magnificence of the repast for most of the morning and when it came to the time for their next breakfast my own fears were validated. For that next morning even more food was laid out for them. In the rural area of Germany concerned it is considered an insult to your guests if the table is clear, it means you have failed and they have left wanting more.

My friends managed to gain approximately 12 pounds in weight during their brief stay.

## It's all in the geography

Depending on where you are eating, please take care with regard to your consumption. In some areas it is considered polite to serve yourself to food and to clear your plate, in other circumstances it may be considered better manners to leave a little on the plate.

The one is a compliment to your host that you have enjoyed their cooking. The other compliments the fact that you have been well fed.

## Running out

If you are the host and you see the courses are not enough then you should explain that you are dieting or, indeed, that you are not overly hungry having prepared it yourself. Thus ensuring that the food will go round all the guests.

### Roland's recommendation

**THOSE TRICKY BITS**

What about those delicate little tit-bits that we all enjoy but few people have the courage to eat in public? Here I mean things I like artichoke, asparagus, crab's claws, mussels, and of course oysters. Fear not, it is with great pleasure I can tell you that it is perfectly acceptable to use your fingers.

However, please, please, resist the temptation to lick your digits afterwards. That is what a finger bowl is for.

## The Italian job

You know what I am about to say, spaghetti! How do we successfully eat spaghetti while retaining some modicum of decency? The answer is simple, we don't! Serve spaghetti when dining with close friends. You can of course use the old method of twisting the fork against the spoon holding the spaghetti but however hard you try you might never totally succeed. Just enjoy it.

## Coffee time

By all means serve coffee at the table, this is quite traditional. You may ask your guests to join you for coffee in the drawing room. Again this is perfectly acceptable and also gives you time to make the coffee and clear most of the dinner detritus from the dining room into the kitchen.

### Roland's recommendation

**AFTER DINNER DRINKS**

My word yes! Provide port, brandy and a liqueur. This will be splendid for any guests. In fact at my own house we have a tradition that after dinner the cork is taken out of the brandy and the port, and is not replaced. This is heroic indeed if there are only four or five for dinner and you will undoubtedly have well-dressed breakfast guests the next morning.

## Any port in a storm

Always remember that if you are serving port, the decanter should be passed around the table in a clockwise direction.

## Time to go home

When it is time for your guests to depart make sure you thank them for their attendance. If the party has been for a special occasion or has had a certain theme why not present them with a small surprise or 'goody' bag to go home with, I always think this a charming touch.

If you have been you must, obviously, thank your hosts. Not only on the departure from their home but also in the next day or so after the function. This may be done by letter or even an acceptable card. We must allow, of course, for the email in this context. At least you have remembered.

# Now to review the situation

- Be ready to greet your guests.
- If you are a guest you need not bring wine. Try bringing good coffee or even flowers.
- Introduce them to each other if necessary.
- Don't leave people standing around, give them a drink, give them nibbles.
- Show them a seating plan. It helps and can look fun.
- Introduce each course to the table, if your table is small encourage your guests to serve themselves, ladies first of course.
- Have you arranged for help? If you have, make sure they are knowledgeable with regard to your courses.
- Make your guests feel that they are the most important part of the evening.
- Check for any special dietary needs. (Vegetarians, etc).
- Clear each course away quickly. Leave a little time between courses, (five minutes or so).
- If you are serving a dessert course clear the table of all others items first, apart from the port and glasses.
- Remember, port is served 'clockwise' around the table.
- Eating cheese from your knife is perfectly good manners.
- Always thank your guests for attending.
- Always thank your hosts for their invitation.

# Ask the professor...

**Q**  *Is it rude to drink whilst still chewing?*

**A**  You should always wait until your mouth is cleared of food before drinking.

**Q**  *What is the correct positioning for a coffee cup?*

**A**  The cup and saucer are placed to the right of the place setting. They should be to the right of the furthest utensil, with the handle of the cup facing the right.

**Q**  *How should I place a large dinner napkin in my lap?*

**A**  Large napkin should, after opening, be folded in half before placing on one's lap.

**Q**  *Is it correct for a woman to apply lipstick at the table after a meal?*

**A**  Certainly not! A lady will excuse herself and apply her lipstick in private.

Every one of us is an artist, and as an artist, you really can stroll into any venue that you want, as long as you take your time to learn the etiquette of that venue.

*Terence Howard*

# Other
# functions

# chapter 6
# **Other functions**

If you enjoy entertaining the range of functions open to you is endless. You don't have to limit yourself to parties of the indoor variety. Why not organise something different?

## The garden party

Perfect for those summer afternoons. All you need is a garden! Try to obtain one of those awfully useful gazebo type tents that are open at the sides but provide shelter from the top. Perfect for laying out food and drink.

### What should you serve?

Bear in mind that the garden party is usually an afternoon affair. Serve tea, of course, and also try iced coffee, perfect for the occasion as is Iced Tea. If your guests are staying on then by all means serve a chilled wine. Nothing too heavy, this is a warm summer day remember!

### And the food?

Again, light, fresh and in tune with a summer function. Try asparagus served simply with brown bread and butter. Potted shrimps or salmon, assorted open savoury pastries and why not throw in a good old fashioned trifle? Don't forget strawberries and cream, or if you want to be different, raspberries. Ah shades of Henley Regatta and "Eight's Week" at Oxford.

# A literary evening

Why not try having an evening with a literary theme? This can be great fun and all a guest needs is the book that you are going to use. This can be anything from Agatha Christie, William Morris or even J.K. Rowling.

## An interesting angle

You can host a party whereby your guests have to come as a designated character from the book. Even more devious is to have each guest arrive and they must simply 'Act' as one of the book's characters but not actually tell anyone who they are. The others must then guess at the end of the evening. Great fun! Treat this like a cheese and wine party. The same rules apply and no fancy dress needed!

# A musical evening

Oh no, dear reader, I am most definitely not telling you to gather around the piano forte whilst Great Aunt Aubretia holds forth in Wagnerian tones thrilling everyone with her rendition of the "Indian Love Lyrics". What I do suggest, however, is a simple supper party with a difference.

## An intimate evening

Invite no more than five or six good friends, this is not a function for strangers, and serve a reasonably light supper. By this I mean a meal of no more than three courses maximum and perhaps food of the 'comfort' variety. I advise something like goulash or a curry followed by a sticky pudding, and cheese and biscuits.

Keep this one informal, let your friends dress casually, this is an intimate evening.

The reason for the intimacy is that each guest must bring a tape containing four pieces of music that are important to them. These are played over your relaxing meal and each guest must explain why they have chosen each piece and why it is important to them. This can make for an enchanting evening, it is something I am very fond of and the intimacy only succeeds in strengthening friendships. A sort of culinary *Desert Island Discs*.

# A progressive or safari dinner

These are enormous fun. The plan is simple, in conjunction with a group of friends make arrangements between yourselves to each cook and serve a course for a formal dinner. You all meet at a given location for pre-dinner drinks and canapés, and then it's on to the next house for the soup/fish course. Proceeding then on to the next for the main course and so on until the night reaches its conclusion.

## The wheel problem

To avoid the problem of driving may I suggest you 'do a deal' with your local mini-cab firm?

## Black tie?

You can actually 'dress for dinner' for this arrangement. It makes it a very special function and it also means that one household does not have the amount of washing up afterwards normally reserved for Genghis Khan's Golden Horde.

# The birthday party

One of the most common this little beast! We all have them. It's only supposed to be once a year but I am certain that the regularity of my own birthdays is increasing as the years go on! If you wish to throw a birthday party properly and here, I am assuming, you do not want to host a dinner party for the event, then the choice is yours.

## Roland's recommendation

**THE RUNNING BUFFET**

I personally think that a buffet is an ideal meal for the more energetic party. By that I mean people milling around and mixing as opposed to being seated. It also means that you can invite more people than you would normally have at a dinner function.

## Out of doors

If the weather is fine why not hold your party in the garden, if the date is late in the year then a simple rearranging of your home's interior will suffice. (Remember what I told you about "battening down the hatches".)

A buffet should be laid either on your dining table (with a cloth on) or on a console table, or tables, along a clear wall. You will need a veritable army of serving dishes and implements to make it a success. Why not, if inviting close friends, ask them to loan dishes and serving spoons etc? There is nothing wrong or rude in asking for help.

## The lubrication question

Again supply a limited variety of drinks, your friends are here to share your birthday, they are not using a hotel bar. As with some of our earlier functions discussed, less is more. Serve a white wine and a red, or perhaps even a rosé. Beer as well is fine, limit yourself to one or two types only. Keep a mixed fruit juice for the drivers and all is well.

# On the plane

In this day and age, many of us are finding that flying is becoming more and more frequent. To remove some of the stress to both yourself and others may I suggest you follow these simple rules?

## Be prepared

When preparing to go through security, please don't wait until you are at the conveyor belt before you are starting to get ready; nothing is more annoying than someone holding up the fellow passengers whilst fumbling with their own items.

## Get it on

You know your seat number, go to it and sit down for heaven's sake. Please do not be one of those that blocks the aisle and stops everyone else getting to their seats.

## Spare a thought

Spare a thought for other travellers using the overhead locker. Remember this is a shared space, however the foot space in front of you is yours.

## The mobile menace

Please, when you are asked, turn your blessed mobile phone off. When the time comes for you to turn them back on again I beg you, bear in mind there are others in the cabin. Not everybody wants to hear your fancy start up tune, latest ring tone or your private business. Keep it off until you disembark the plane.

## The laptop

Remember they can make a noise. It might annoy if you use your laptop to play games, there is after all a sound control. Spare a thought for others.

## Reclining

When it is safe for you to recline your seat, or use the tray in front of you, do so carefully. Remember there is someone sitting behind you and if you jerk your seat back they are likely to end up with a lap full of tea or worse, coffee. Again, think of others.

## The classic bore

I can think of nothing worse than being virtually a captive to the bore next to you. The same applies to you, please don't force your conversation on others.

## Getting out of it

If the person next to you is slowly numbing your brains with their full and exceptionally dreary life story, it is perfectly acceptable to inform them that you are feeling tired or a little unwell and therefore not willing to talk at that point. Don't be rude, it could be that they are merely nervous fliers.

## Making a stand

When standing please, please avoid pulling yourself up by grabbing the seat in front of you. How many times has this happened to you? It's annoying isn't it?

## The conference passenger

Why do some people insist on having a business meeting across the aisle of the plane? Wait until you get there! (How can you be sure the person behind you isn't a rival?)

## Something off the trolley

If the flight attendant is trying to serve food and beverage, please do not hinder them. Let the attendant and their cart move freely down the plane.

## Having a tipple

At high altitudes the effect of alcohol can be magnified. Take care what you drink.

## Getting off

Have you ever noticed that when the plane taxis to its final halt the flight attendant always ask that people remain seated until the seatbelt lights are switched off before you stand and remove your bags from the overhead locker. Why then does no one take any notice? You won't get off any quicker and you will only succeed in annoying others. Please do as you are told, it is simply common courtesy.

Know, first,
who you are;
and then adorn
yourself accordingly.

*Epictetus*

# Dressing
## the part

# chapter 7
# Dressing the part

It has been said that "clothes maketh the man", this, to some extent is true. However, if you wear the clothes then behave accordingly. I know many wealthy people who can afford the best in attire but their bearing sets them apart from the gentleman or lady.

## Roland's recommendation

**KEEP IT TRADITIONAL**
Gentlemen, and ladies too, remember that when dressing for an occasion "less is more". Traditional styling and classics can say more about you on your first meeting than going over the top with cat walk extravaganzas.

## Ladies and hats – a timeless combination

Ladies, when you are attending a function that needs a hat, take care. There is a fine balance between elegance, or even extravagance, and the downright absurd.

## The plane! The plane!

A large picture hat can look stunning but it should also be manageable. One would not like to imagine the effect of strong winds elevating not your social status but your entire person. Mary Poppins perfected flying, you however might only prove a danger to low flying aircraft.

## On the square

The silk head-square, or scarf, is a timeless item for ladies to own. Perfect for shopping in the provinces and an absolute must for any equestrian event. Please though, tie it well; nothing detracts from a lady's charms than her resembling a Tuareg tribesman.

## That 'country' look

If you are spending time in the country you can't go wrong with tweed. Ladies and gentlemen both benefit from its comfort and durability. Choose well, try different cuts and experiment with the look you are searching for.

## The smell of heather

That old favourite "Harris Tweed" is still the doyen of the country wardrobe. Coming, as it does, from the Isle of Lewis it is said that you should still smell the heather on its surface when it is purchased.

### Roland's recommendation

**COMBINATIONS**

No, I do not refer to that most unflattering of undergarments but rather the permutations of dress you can achieve by mixing and matching the clothes you wear. Tweed jackets look good with trousers, kilts, skirts, and even jeans for that that slightly more modern look.

## Cavalry dash!

Cavalry tweeds are available in an assortment of colours and most look equally good with a sports coat or even a blazer. A deep red can look very good when teamed with a blazer and is even acceptable for town use.

## The "wooly pully"

Ah, the comfort and warmth of school that stays with us all our lives. Here the choice is endless. A military style pullover with elbow and shoulder patches is superb in any colour and we must not forget our old friend the cricket sweater. This garment is warm and easily blends into casual wear, it also looks jolly good for ladies too, you don't have to be a Len Hutton to carry it off; (Len Hutton, now that dates me!),

# Get a head, get a hat

For country use, the ubiquitous cloth cap is still as favoured as ever and again both ladies and gentlemen can achieve the desired look from this simple garment. Choose a make like "Christie's" for the best cut, one does not want to end up looking like an off duty refuse disposal operative. (That's a dustman if you wondered).

## The Panama

My favourite type of head wear. You can get plain 'Trilby' straw types, cream coloured material types and of course, the ultimate and genuine, the 'Fold Flat Panama' itself.

This simply shouts out 'summer, cricket, and the gentleman'.

## Fore and aft

Here I refer to the tweed hat that has peaks both front and rear. The 'Deer stalker' is still popular but I personally prefer the 'Ghillie' it lacks the ear flaps and sits more comfortably. Of course, a trilby still holds court and is usable also in town if you become an inveterate titfer wearer.

## The bowler

This hat is the crowning glory of the hatter's art. Certainly it is one of the most expensive but its appearance reeks of class. It is worn in the country at show events and by those participating in equestrian events. It is, however, in the city that this hat displays its true form.

## Who still wears them?

Anyone cutting a dash. City workers, off duty guards officers and gentlemen who have cultivated its use. It should however only be worn by Englishmen. It is not advisable for anyone from a foreign nationality to attempt its wearing and, indeed, if a Frenchman should do so it should be considered a crime punishable by the most heinous penalties!

## The "baseball" cap

This has now become part of the average wardrobe. Indeed, a great many sporting clubs have adopted its use in their clothing needs. As the years progress we must make allowances and therefore we must allow its entry into our list of hats, but only with the most casual clothing.

## The "cowboy" hat

Dear Lord what are you thinking! May one ask if you are desirous of forming a 'line dancing' club or perhaps one shops at supermarkets with a western saddled horse outside?

## The "topper"

Very rarely do we ever find a hat of such elegance. Whether it is of the grey felt variety or the polished black silk these hats ooze style, elegance, and charm. They hark back to Edwardian times and unfortunately are not worn enough, in my opinion.

Charmingly enough, one can still see these hats worn in a day to day use if you go into Germany and view the chimney sweeps there. The houses in Germany are still built with metal brackets on the outside walls to enable the sweep to climb the outside of the building. Here the sweep cleans the chimney from the top and thence downwards.

His black silk Topper is complemented by a double breasted black tail coat and to see one is still considered very lucky.

These gentlemen are still in great demand at weddings and a large 'sooty' kiss from these men is still regarded as a sign of a long and happy marriage.

### Roland's recommendation

**CORD HATS AND CAPS**
Never, ever! Avoid these like a drink from the 'Cosa Nostra'. Enough said!

# In the city

If we are spending any time in the city then we must change our wardrobe accordingly. Remember the old adage "no brown in town".

For gentlemen choose the smarter type of city suit; greys and blues or stripes of a subtle nature. Whether single or double breasted the choice is yours. Excellent 'Off The Peg' suits are available to purchase, or you can be measured for a suit, jacket or blazer. This is the ultimate for your wardrobe.

Many firms such as Gieves and Hawkes in the city can help. You can choose your cloth and then the item is made for you. What could be more perfect?

## Blaze away

The Blazer has become a perfectly acceptable form of attire in the city, although one should not use it for business purposes. It is fine for less formal affairs and for that American interloper "Dress down Fridays". It is also perfect for sporting events and museums/galleries.

## Scots wahey!

Ladies, be thrilled, the kilt can still hold sway in the city. Worn teamed with the twin set it provides a perfectly acceptable accompaniment to the city wardrobe. For gentlemen too if you are of Scottish extract. But only on occasions that dictate its use or leave it acceptable for you do so.

## Denim classics

Jeans, you might be pleased to hear, are now becoming more and more presentable when worn in the city. Never for business but for casual wear. They can look good on the younger man if matched with the blazer or the sports coat. Please, however, try to avoid looking like a refugee from the Glastonbury Festival. Use a classic cut like the Levi 501 style and always make sure they are not of the 'ripped' variety. Casual is one thing, resembling an outcast from a boy-band is quite another.

### Roland's recommendation

**THAT LEATHER LOOK**

A leather jacket has become more and more used in town over the past years. Again choose a classic style. Avoid using the 'Biker' type unless you actually own a motor bicycle. The leather jacket gives the feeling of rebellion and can look good on certain people, gentlemen and ladies. However, bear in mind that no matter what you might think, you probably will not look like Marlon Brando in "The Wild One", you might pass easier as an owner of the seedier type of club in Soho. (Or so I'm told!)

## The dinner suit

For a man this can be the most flattering garment. Again they are available in a variety of styles but you should try to restrict yourself to the basic black version. Dinner suits in greens and blues somehow miss the point. Stay traditional, you will only ever purchase one or two in your life, make it a wise purchase.

## The black tie

This means what it says. For formal dinners and functions you will be invited to wear 'Black Tie' this means dinner suit with a dress shirt and black bow tie. Please purchase the type that you have to tie yourself, ready-made bows are simply not on. If you practise you can do it, I have faith in you. Remember it should not look perfect, mine never does, it shows you have done it yourself. Congatulations!

## The shirt

The dress shirt for evening functions is a work of art. Choose pleats for style and if you wish use one that has dress studs, very elegant. It should have a double cuff and must be used with cuff links. A wing collar can add a touch of dash if you wish, I have both and enjoy the 'wingers' as the bow seems to sit better on the collar. And one quick word, never, ever, frills! 70s disco fashion is not, repeat, not acceptable.

## The day shirt

Whether worn with a suit or something more casual, the day shirt should complement the outfit. Spend a little more than normal on these items. Always try to purchase one that can take cuff links, the finishing touch. Firms such as Thomas Pink in St James' provide excellent shirts and also operate a first class mail order service. Whether plain or stripes, a good shirt provides a superb flourish to your outfit.

## The tie

Many people now have taken to wearing suits with open neck shirts, this is simply being lazy. Choose a good quality tie and wear it. Club ties are excellent for providing colour and show your allegiance to an organisation or sporting body. Regimental ties as well show that touch of class in an otherwise drab era.

### Roland's recommendation

**TYING THE THING**

Tie your chosen neckwear with care. It should flow from the neck and not look as though it is attempting to constrict your airway, neither should it be so loose as to hang like some limp rodent that has expired around your neck.

# Footy

For ladies and gentlemen the shoe is the item that finishes off the outfit to perfection. You can ruin all your hard work by wearing cheap or ill chosen shoes.

## Selection

For the gentleman you do not need a huge range for a good wardrobe. A pair of polished black toe cap shoes is essential. You may use these for city or evening wear. Black loafers make a pleasant alternative for a slightly less formal dinner.

## Suppliers

I have always found that "Clifford James" of Skelmersdale have always stocked a superb range of classical footwear for gentlemen and ladies. If you do feel particularly flush you can always use "Lobbs" of Saint James' of course!

## Something more rustic

A pair of black semi brogues is perfect for use with a suit or when wearing a blazer in its more formal sense. Brown full brogues are best for country wear and a pair in suede are magnificent for attending sporting engagements such as cricket matches. Again try "Clifford James".

## That Paddington touch

Don't forget your wellies. Ladies and gentlemen should have at least one pair. The green 'Hunters' are superb, however I must give you a word of caution. A few years ago I bought a new pair of 'Royal Hunters', those with the metal studs on the sole. Really rather good for country use but imagine my surprise when, after wearing them in the aftermath of a heavy snow fall, I entered Sainsbury's and found myself propelled along the wine aisle by the studs reacting with the polished tiles.

## Something more dainty

Ladies do not need any help from me in purchasing shoes. The essence of Imelda Marcos is alive and well. Court shoes, day shoes, slingbacks. Go on ladies, you've earned it!

## Accoutrements

Always have umbrellas to hand. They not only keep the rain off but they are invaluable for hailing taxis.

# Personal jewellery

Yet again "less is more". Keep things simple to achieve that elegant balance.

## Rings for his finger

A simple signet ring worn on the little finger is very elegant in itself. This can contain either your family crest or a monogram of your initials.

On the ring finger of the right hand a larger ring is also acceptable but please take care. The 'Sovereign Ring' is not a subtlety and the habit of some people of wearing rings on every finger available only adds to the confusion between themselves and a rather large, dark gentleman from 'The "A" Team'.

## It's the ladies' turn

Yours is the greatest choice. For everyday use most ladies involved in a marriage, or some similar form of co-habitation, will make do with an engagement ring, a wedding and perhaps an eternity ring. A dress ring or, indeed, a signet ring, completes the package on the other hand.

When out and about however then the jewellery box is yours. Do not, however, overdo it. Again, your fingers may contain diamonds but should not imitate small chandeliers.

## The earring

For ladies perfect, for gentlemen slightly less so. A lady can wear and should wear earrings fitted for the occasion. I am certain none of you would attend Ascot in 8 inch gold loops with tiger skin tails trailing over your shoulders.

Gentlemen please be more subtle. A stud if you must, a small ring if you must but please leave it there. Very few of you will be rock stars of the more obvious type. Please dress accordingly.

### Roland's recommendation

**TATTOOS?**
Apart from the annual variety at Edinburgh Castle, I mean 'body art'. I have seen some varieties that look very artistic. A word of caution, they are permanent. If you must have one have it done where it is normally out of sight. Many people find their appearance unacceptable.

The normal "Love and Hate" on ones knuckles is out of the question! I have even seen "Cut Here" emblazoned on a throat. I offer no further comment.

## Body piercings?

Shudder the thought. This is not that sort of book!

# Watching it!

There are many excellent wristwatches available for both ladies and gentlemen. Once again the choice is yours. You may choose from either those with a metal bracelet or those that are held in place by a leather strap, either way the only caution I give is this: let it tell the time. It will hardly be either elegant or stylish for your wrist to be weighted down with some monstrosity that resembles a chiming goldfish bowl and that every hour on the hour makes soup and microwaves your arm!

# The links

A cuff link finishes a shirt perfectly. There are numerous styles to choose from. They do not have to be silver or gold; some very pleasant enamel 'links' are available and they can look very good in dress shirts.

If you do wish to purchase gold or silver cuff links then why not have them engraved with your initials or even your family crest, if you have one? It would be best however to avoid those that are large and overly endowed with fake gem-stones. The look to cultivate is elegance, not that of a New York Pimp!

# The stick pin

The stick pin or tie pin is not much used these days. One of the main reasons of course is that it damages the tie when the pin is stuck through. That said, it can be a very attractive addition to formal wear, in particular if you are wearing a morning coat and therefore a formal cravat. An elegant pin is perfect for setting off the ensemble.

# Additional items

## The cummerbund

I have left this item until now as so many people are still confused as to what one is. The cummerbund is Indian in origin and dates back to the days of the British Raj.

It is a sash of silk that is carefully folded around the waist to hide the join between the evening dress shirt and the trouser band of your dress trousers. In fact, the cummerbund was originally pleated and it was common to keep you pocket watch in its folds. Remember when you put it on, (and it tends to be ready-tied these days), that the folds are open to the top. All in all, a very elegant accoutrement.

## Braces – that's suspenders for the US!

A most useful tool for the man. Trousers are designed to fit well and hang perfectly. If you are wearing the same pair of trousers for some hours, you run the risk of them riding down. This is sloppy and shows scant respect for your tailor!

Braces are a first class way of keeping the trouser hanging just right. They should skirt the shoe and not be hovering above, nor should they be rumpled up in great creases over the shoe. Your escort is going to be dressed superbly I feel sure, you owe it to yourself to do your part.

# The hirsute question

Ladies all know the importance of excellence in the field of grooming and hair. Some gentlemen I'm afraid do not. A good haircut goes without saying but what about beards and moustaches?

If you are cultivating facial hair and, I hope, I'm talking to the gentlemen, you must keep it well trimmed. There is nothing so unbecoming as a hedgerow attached to your face. Apart from anything else, or so I'm told, it makes things a little uncomfortable for your nearest and dearest!

"Trumpers" in Albemarle Street, Saint James' carry excellent grooming products.

## Some points to bear in mind

- Always choose a classical style. You can still customise it to make it your own.
- In the country use tweeds and associated materials.
- Heavier shirts are good for country use.
- Footwear should be substantial and well made. Don't forget the wellies.
- In town clothing should be lighter. No brown in town!
- A good tailor will supply you with a selection of city suits. Go for blues and greys.
- Well-made shirts are important. Pay more and get better!
- Use cuff links where possible.
- Keep a selection of ties to hand. Club ties are good.
- Your shoes for the city should be lighter and of a more polished finish.
- Keep a selection of hats for use in town and country.
- Kilts are still 'in'.
- Keep jewellery subtle and understated. It should complement not overshadow.
- If you have facial hair, keep it trimmed.
- Your watch should tell the time and complement your outfit. Avoid the 'Chunk'.
- Large gold 'I.D.' bracelets are not suitable for gentlemen. They are merely ostentatious.
- A Tattoo? If you insist keep it hidden. Keep it subtle.

# Ask the professor...

**Q** *When at a department store, who gets on or off an elevator first when the doors open; is it the people in the elevator or the people waiting for the elevator?*

**A** Wait until all passengers have exited the elevator before attempting to enter. This is particularly true during a store's sale time. We all know that tempers run high on such occasions.

**Q** *Is it appropriate for someone to ask you to remove your shoes when entering their home?*

**A** Yes, when you are a guest in someone's home you should abide by their rules and requests. Interestingly, it is very common in most Swedish houses for people to remove their shoes before entering.

**Q** *When in a restaurant is it customary to leave a tip?*

**A** This depends on geography. Seek local advice, for instance, in Iceland it is insulting to tip a waiter.

The man who can dominate a London dinner-table can dominate the world.

*Oscar Wilde*

# Out and about

# chapter 8
# Out and about

**W**hen you are mixing freely in society and here I mean any society, make sure that your behaviour is easily non-recognisable. A strange thing to state but perfect manners and decorum should not appear staged and should flow un-noticed. Then you know you have got it right.

## Restaurant etiquette

### Timing is everything

Reservations at some restaurants are as difficult to get as unicorn droppings. Therefore always remember if you have a reservation stick to it. Treat it like any other business appointment.

### Roland's recommendation

**BEING LATE**

If you are going to be in excess of fifteen minutes late then phone ahead and inform the restaurant. If you fail to do this you might lose your table!

### The all important dress code

These days it is rare to find a restaurant that still expects the diners to wear a jacket let alone black tie. There are some of us who miss the formality. However, these changes have made restaurant dining far more amenable to a wider clientele.

## Going casual

The meaning of casual can vary from person to person. However if you are dining in a restaurant with a good reputation and locale, then dress accordingly. When in doubt choose the conservative option.

## Choices from the menu

If you are dining with your partner, especially if it is early in your relationship and you wish to create a good impression, why not ask "Would you like me to order for you?". This is best done where you are known at the restaurant and know the staff.

### Roland's recommendation

**SUFFERING IN SILENCE**

What do you do if your food or the food of your dinner guest is not properly cooked? Don't suffer in silence. By all means complain but do so politely yet firmly. Remember it is not the waiter who has cooked the food but bear in mind if you are rude it is the waiter who will be alone with your food.

## The other side of the coin

On the flip side, if your meal has been good and the service also, make sure that you compliment the staff.

## Mobile phones

These machines have their uses but can be pure anathema in a social or dining environment. I sincerely hope that if you were at home eating with your family you would not answer your mobile phone, please observe the same courtesy in a restaurant. Other people do not wish to hear your conversation while dining.

### Roland's recommendation

**THE WINE QUESTION**

If you are not a wine expert never hesitate to ask for the opinion of a wine waiter; a good wine waiter, if you inform him of your needs, will always suggest the correct bottle. It is in the interests of the restaurant to do this.

## Corking it

You do not need to be an expert to know when a wine is corked. It smells like a mixture between vinegar and damp linoleum. The taste is no better should you get past the smell stage. Do not hesitate to return bad wine.

## What about the kiddy-winks?

It is never too early to introduce children to restaurants and thereby to good manners when in public. Do bear in mind, however, that poorly behaved children will ruin the dining experience of your fellow restaurant goers. Therefore ensure they behave correctly.

## Roland's recommendation

**THE DOGGY BAG**

There is absolutely nothing wrong with taking home a doggy bag. Many restaurants these days produce far more food than a normal human can consume at one sitting. It is a compliment to the chef to ask for a doggy bag, as the food is obviously so good you do not want to waste any of it.

## Tipping

A general rule of thumb for tipping waiting staff is approximately 15–20% of the bill. This varies from country to country, investigate upon your arrival.

## Talk to your waiter

If the restaurant is new to you, or indeed you are new to that country, talk to your waiter. You can quickly build a relationship that will ensure good service and a desire to dine there again.

A good restaurant can make a distant place feel like home.

# Gentleman's etiquette

## It's a lip thing!

"A kiss on the hand may be quite continental", so they say but please gentlemen treat the occasion as a slight brushing of the lips on the ladies hand, try to avoid the "Slobber" at all costs.

## A genteel greeting please

If greeting a lady of your acquaintance with whom you are well known and to some extent 'intimate', it is perfectly acceptable to GENTLY embrace by placing your hands on her shoulders and placing your cheeks against hers in a 'kissing' gesture.

Please avoid grabbing hold of the poor unfortunate lady in a bear hug whilst proclaiming loudly "Hello Alice, how's your bum for paw prints"!

## Street wise

It might be old fashioned but if you are a gentleman please walk on the outside of the lady when in the street. By this I mean place yourself between her and the edge of the road.

It dates back to the days when a carriage might splash mud on the ladies gown from the gutter, admittedly that is unlikely now but the gesture remains constant.

### Roland's recommendation

**ON YOUR FEET**

Again, it might seem obvious but you would be surprised how many times I have seen this forgotten. If a lady enters or leaves a room, please stand. It is also the same when a lady arrives at or leaves the dinner table. Stand and wait for her to be seated or leave the room.

# An anecdote

## A down-under thing

Some years ago, whilst touring in Australia, (it's not that they do more of this type of thing, it's just that they do it so well!) I was invited to a cocktail party held at one of the government buildings in Eastern Australia. The guests were a gallimauphry (yes, that is a real word) of Australian society.

The evening progressed well, the drinks flowed and the warm evening breeze caressed the partygoers with the gentle drift of its breath just causing a faint stirring in the bushes of the formal gardens.

It became obvious to me, however, that some of the ladies who were in attendance had perhaps imbibed not wisely but well for as the night drew on the accents of some of the said ladies became a little broader than in previous moments and somewhat considerably louder.

One particular lady, of the type that only Australia can produce and certainly a person who had enough front and courage to tackle "Dame Edna" head-on, became particularly vocal but in the most enchanting and amusing way. Now I had certainly heard of the wonderful cocktail the "Tom Collins", as I'm sure had this lady, but to my amusement and certainly to the added mirth of the other party goers, she proceeded to tell the young barman, in a loud and clear tone, "What I'd really like right now is a nice long cold John Thomas"!

Cocktail parties have never been the same since. I do hope she became very successful.

# Chivalry

Actually, not too long ago, this simple act of courtesy secured me a job. I was asked into the office of the person with whom I had the appointment and after around ten minutes the door opened and in came his secretary.

I stood as she entered and then opened the door as she was about to leave. I was then informed that I had the contract I was seeking. The particular 'Don' with whom I was in interview, then told me that he had instructed his secretary to enter at this stage with all the previous interviewees and I had been the only one to show her the respect due.

It still counts. It's still important and it can still be seen as such.

# Trains and boats and planes

This might sound a little strange but have you ever considered good manners on public transport? When boarding a bus or train the gentleman should always let the lady board first offering his arm to assist in her carriage.

When leaving the same vehicle it is the man who alights first in order to again lend his hand to the lady. It's common sense really, so why do so few people do this?

A while ago whilst journeying in the provinces I had cause to use a rather over-filled railway train. As the stations were all halted at and more and still more people boarded the train I noticed a young lady standing close by.

Unfortunately I did not realise that an act of courtesy could cause offence! As I offered her my seat, the young lady …

... retorted with the rather acidly delivered comment "I hope you're not doing this because I'm a woman"!

Fractionally taken aback I however responded with "No madam, I think I am doing it because I'm a gentleman".

## Winging it

When travelling by aircraft, if you find yourself travelling next to a young lady who is apparently travelling alone, then please offer to assist with the overhead baggage. It takes only a second of your time and yet you would be astonished how many times I have seen the male of the species watching a lady struggle and not offering any attempt at all. Content instead to bury his nose in the latest copy of "Nuts" magazine.

## Restoration opportunities

Over the last few years I have witnessed a marked decline in gentlemanly conduct. I hear it said time and again that "The age of the gentleman is dead", I think it time to restore the reputation of the male and attempt to ensure that once again we can be viewed as 'gentlemen'!

### Roland's recommendation

**A DUCHESS AT EVERY CORNER**
A very great gentleman once told me "Treat every lady you meet like a duchess until she tells you or shows you differently". Something I have always kept in mind.

## And ladies please…

As we gentlemen try to recapture the age of chivalry, if you find it difficult to handle and feel a bit rebellious then please take it out on a stiffer than usual martini or a particularly violent flower arrangement.

# Race day etiquette

When attending a normal 'Race Meet' most gentlemen are usually comfortable in a 'Country' suit. This is generally of some kind of check and topped with a trilby of some colour. Have you ever tried wearing a blue shirt with a tweed suit? It looks really good. A comfortable day dress for ladies and if chilly try wearing the ever faithful wax jacket. All topped off with your favourite head scarf, super!

## Roland's recommendation

**PLACE YOUR BETS!**
A gentleman should always place the bet for the lady, it's considered bad form for a lady to stand in line for a 'bookie'.

# Lunch

If you are travelling in a party and you don't want to use the dining facilities at the race-course, some of which can be very expensive, then this is the ideal time for the picnic. Even in colder weather this can be fun. Use lots of cold sausages with plenty of dips. Why not make large thermos flasks of mulled wine? Super stuff.

# An anecdote

## A sense of occasion

It is indeed a fact that our own dear Royal Family are passionately fond of horse racing. It is after all the "Sport of Kings". Some years ago at Windsor Castle – that monument to everything that is Britain with a thousand years of our heritage being encased within its glowering walls – there was a formal ball being held, the occasion and meaning now escape me.

As is right and proper, all the guests were lined up in order of importance to make their entrance into the ballroom. The sight was stunning indeed, the gentlemen clad in white tie and tails, that magnificent reminder of earlier days when Astaire and Rogers thrilled us with their movements.

The ladies all clad in the most glittering of ball gowns, tiaras aplenty and orders shining on the material of the gowns like a glistening frost on a midwinter morning.

As we all stood to make our entrance, the truly great lady on my arm looked at me with a wry smile and said "Here we go, Roly, under starters orders"! The perfect thing for this wonderful lady to say, I am only sorry that she is no longer with us. God Bless you Ma'am!

## Roland's recommendation

**ENTERING INTO THE SPIRIT**
Get excited, it's all part of the fun. I have seen people of all stages in life leaping around like pan fried whitebait, there's nothing wrong with it. Who can forget Eliza Doolittle's outburst in "My Fair Lady"? Simply charming.

## The polo match

This is one of the most exciting and exhilarating games that you can possibly witness. It is fast and furious, and of course, a highlight of any social calendar.

The dress for a polo match is very similar to that of a race meeting. If the weather is fine, day dress for ladies and something suitable for gentlemen.

The interesting part of the match however, is the audience participation during the intervals of play.  When these intervals occur, the spectators are encouraged to take to the field and walk the pitch in doing so treading down the pieces of turf that have become dislodged during the game.

Not only an enjoyable but useful additional activity to the day's proceedings. Don't forget ladies, this is yet another excuse for a hat!

# Theatre etiquette

If visiting the theatre it tends to be more common these days for people to dress reasonably casually. Trends change and we must accept, however, if you are told it is to be a formal theatre engagement then it tends to be 'black tie' for men and 'cocktail dress' for ladies.

## Pre-theatre

It is a good idea to dine first. After a performance you might fall foul of "Chucking Out Time" and the restaurants and streets might contain the element of person that your good lady might not appreciate.

## Roland's recommendation

**THE SNIFTER**

Gentlemen, don't forget to order your partner's half-time drink before you enter the auditorium, it will take ages if you try to purchase during the interval.

## The performance

Again, get involved. The play is there to entertain and transport you for a brief while into another world. By getting involved emotionally you are complimenting the actors on their ability. It's as good as an Oscar.

# An anecdote

## A delightful shock

I recall that a little while ago, I was working in Birmingham at the time in question, one of my colleagues, who had not embraced the fine arts at all, asked me what my plans were for the coming weekend. I informed him I was going to Stratford-upon-Avon to see "King Lear"; "Who's he then?" came the reply. I explained that King Lear was in fact a play by Shakespeare and not a visiting dignitary.

My colleague was somewhat taken aback, it transpired he had never been to the theatre and never witnessed a performance of the illustrious bard. I offered to take him and we duly booked into a very nice little hotel of my acquaintance.

After an early dinner we decamped to the Royal Shakespeare Theatre and soon were engrossed in the performance. It reached the point in the play when Lear's elder daughter was being particularly Machiavellian and plotting her father's commitment as insane. The next thing I knew, my friend leapt to his feet, pointed dramatically at the stage and in a stentorian tone called out "You bloody cow!"

He froze as he realised what he had done and all eyes were upon him as he slowly sank back into his seat with just the tip of his head visible. There were numerous titters around the auditorium and as I looked at the stage, Lear's daughter had the faintest smile playing on her lips. What finer compliment, her performance had so enraptured my friend and so enmeshed was he in the stunning portrayal we were witnessing that he had completely forgotten his surroundings. He accompanied me again on numerous occasions, though not with the same theatrical and embarrassing result.

# International etiquette

Due to lower air fares in recent years, it is now possible for us to travel extensively abroad. However, we must be on our guard; what is considered acceptable behaviour in our own country could be classed as a monumental faux pas in others.

In spite of our belief that our way is the only way, we must not behave like so many foreign visitors when abroad. With a little courtesy we can show our respect for foreign cultures and attempt to integrate into the society that we are visiting.

Please remember when abroad, if your English is not understood, it is not acceptable to respond by merely speaking English in a louder tone of voice. Don't be boorish.

When mixing with society in another country please try to read beforehand any customs that are acceptable and, more importantly, any that are reviled. In other words please let us avoid acting like the "knotted hanky" brigade or, even more appallingly, the football supporter of the vilest excesses.

- Whereas in Europe and indeed, most of the world, the thumbs up sign is generally taken as meaning all is well, this is not a case in the most Latin American countries. Indeed, in Brazil this is perceived as a particularly abhorrent gesture and should be avoided.

- There can be few countries in the world as beautiful as Africa. Its scenery is breathtaking and its people as warm as the sunshine. In direct contrast to Europe however, it is not taboo to discuss a lady's weight. Indeed to inform a lady she has gained a few pounds is very often seen as a compliment to good health.

- On the same continent it should also be observed that children will quite often avoid eye contact with their elders. In Africa it is seen as a sign of respect as opposed to north America where it is generally seen as a sign of guilt.

- If you are travelling in Japan it can sometimes be perceived as a sign of embarrassment or discomfort if you laugh in the company of others. We might consider this strange, but then again I feel certain our own idiosyncrasies appear strange to many foreign visitors to our country.

- Always try to remember when travelling in Southeast Asia that exposing the soles of your feet is considered an extremely rude gesture. Keep your shoes on!

- In Japan when bowing, never turn your eyes down. Bow whilst maintaining eye contact.

- In North Africa never take the last date from a dish, should dates be offered to you. Removing the last item of food from the dish is considered bad manners.

- The people in Sweden also consider it bad manners to have the last of anything left on the plate. I cannot tell you how this annoys me, especially as I have many Swedish visitors.

- If you are invited to attend a wedding or anniversary in Germany, Austria, Switzerland, or indeed anywhere in central Europe, never be the first to dance. This should only be done by the couple celebrating that day; others may dance only after the couple have made one revolution of the dance floor.

- In any country, never, ever, pick your nose in public!

# Interview etiquette

It maybe of use to give you some idea as to the acceptable behaviour and dress code applicable to job interviews. Please note these same rules apply when making an application to a university. Confirming a point upon receipt of your interview letter, or indeed, a letter inviting you to apply, never be afraid to acknowledge the correspondence yourself.

## Preparation is everything

Find out all you can about your prospective employer or university. Use the internet.

## Dress rehearsal

Ask someone to give you a mock interview. Brush up on your techniques. Rehearse answers to any questions that you think might be asked. Carry extra copies of your CV with you.

### Roland's recommendation

**FIRST IMPRESSIONS**
Always remember to visit the restroom to check your appearance before your interview. It is also wise to take a few moments and ensure you are calm before entering.

## The lion's den

As you enter make sure you are smiling. Walk confidently to your interviewer/interviewers, shake hands and introduce yourself. Always wait to be invited before you sit down.

## A sip to calm the nerves

If you are asked to partake in a cup of tea of coffee, always accept. This gives something for your nervous hands to hold during your interview.

## Relax

Sit well back in your chair, relax and give off an air of confidence. Do not tap your feet, waggle your legs, or fiddle with your fingers or clothing.

## Blow your own trumpet

Speak clearly and with confidence. Avoid putting your hands near your face; if you feel you must make hand gestures keep them limited and only use an open palm gesture. It is indeed best to keep your hands folded when not in use. Speak with enthusiasm about your own achievements and your ability as you see it to fill the role they have advertised.

## Stage fright?

If you are overcome with this distemper, concentrate on one interviewer only and pretend that it is a one on one interview. Always remember an interview is an open dialogue, so don't be afraid to ask questions.

## Whipping the old donkey

Never ever speak ill of your employer – current or previous. This does not earn you any brownie points!

## Finishing

At the end of the interview stand, smile, and before leaving thank the interviewers for their time.

### Roland's recommendation

**FRESH IN THE MIND**
Never be afraid to write a letter thanking the interviewer/interviewers for their time; this not only shows courtesy but also keeps you fresh in their minds.

# Supermarket etiquette

If it is forced upon you to attend the daily grind of shopping at any one of our supermarket chains, bear these few morsels in mind and it could make the experience less painful.

## Shades of Boudicca

If you are searching for items in an aisle please keep your trolley with you. Never abandon these vehicles of torture (have you ever noticed that at least one wheel will insist on travelling in an entirely different direction from the others) this only makes it more difficult for other shoppers.

## Restrain yourself

Try to maintain an even temperament. Certainly other shoppers might be dragging you to distraction but I urge control and restraint in all things.

## A matter of control

If you must take your children with you do try to monitor their behaviour. Occasionally children can misbehave in supermarkets, much to the annoyance of other shoppers. Think of others. And attempt bribery, restrained violence, or the use of prescribed drugs in controlled quantities! (I do most sincerely hope that at this point you have realised I have a sense of humour.)

## Checking out time

When you are going through a checkout (I have been told that is what they are called) don't leave your trolley behind you. This only serves to block the way for all other shoppers, remember they aren't having fun either.

# Telephone etiquette

Always remember, using the telephone correctly is one of those hot areas of modern communications. It should therefore be treated with the same regard towards etiquette that we show to other more traditional methods of communication.

## Flying blind

Bear in mind, that every time you speak to someone using the telephone, it is the sound of your voice that portrays the picture of the person. Using the telephone is like flying blind, you can make the direction but you can't see the heading.

## Roland's recommendation

**BE COMFORTABLE**

I have heard many people use the phrase 'smile when you dial', personally I can think of nothing worse than forcing and an inane grin on to an unwilling face. It is certainly true that you can hear if someone is smiling whilst using the telephone, however, it is also possible to hear if their face is contorted into some horrific grimace.

Be comfortable, don't be a gargoyle!

## Clear and precise

For heaven's sake, speak clearly; by this I mean that the person listening should be able to hear your every word without having to ask you to repeat yourself. Don't mumble, don't chew and be precise.

## A good listener

It is also important for you to listen to the person on the other end of the telephone. Don't interrupt, let them finish their sentences before replying. It is only showing the same courtesy that you would in a normal face to face conversation.

# To summarise

- A gentleman walks on the outside of the lady. This protects the lady from the roadside.

- Kissing the hand is a subtle gesture not 'a meal'. A gentle caress is acceptable, a 'grope' is not!

- Make going to the theatre an occasion. Enter into the spirit of the performance. Don't be afraid of showing your emotions. This is a compliment for the actor.

- Take dinner prior to the performance. This avoids the crowds afterwards.

- If attending an outdoor event, take a picnic. This can be fun even in cooler weather. Cold sausages and mulled wine perhaps?

- At the races a gentleman should place the lady's bet.

- Cocktail parties are great fun. Lounge suit for men, cocktail dress for ladies.

- Gentlemen stand for ladies. Give up your seat, help with luggage.

- A gentleman lets a lady onto a train first, assisting her. He is the first to alight when getting off, assisting the lady again.

- Keep hold of the supermarket trolley, it is not your friend. Ditto children.

- Interview first impressions count so check your zipper.

- Remember, on the telephone, out of sight does not mean out of manners.

Treat every woman
you meet like a
duchess until she
tells you or until she
shows you differently.

*Erich von Shiel*

# The royal occasion

# chapter 9
# The royal occasion

Congratulations, you've finally made it and you're going to meet the Royal family. Be on your guard, disasters loom at every turn.

## The meeting

When meeting a female member of the Royal family, if you are male, you will be required to take the royal hand and bow accordingly as if kissing the proffered hand. DON'T YOU DARE!

You only bow that way, your face never comes into contact with the royal person. If you are a lady you will be required to curtsey. This involves just a slight 'bob' with one leg behind the other, not a yoga posture.

## Roland's recommendation

**HOW LOW CAN YOU GO?**

If you are male please do not bend so low as if inspecting their shoes. The possibilities of one's back locking into place reigns supreme, the same must be said for the curtsey.

Nothing could be so embarrassing than being carried from the royal presence by those dear St John's people, and always bear in mind that the 'Royals' rarely travel in public with an attendant chiropractor.

# Do I speak?

Yes, most certainly, but only if you are spoken to first. Your first address to the Queen should be to "Your Majesty" then afterwards as "Ma'am", and it's "Ma'am" as in 'smarm', not "Ma'am" as in 'jam'.

To a royal duke or prince the address is "Your Royal Highness" first and afterwards "Sir". A royal duchess or princess is likewise "Your Royal Highness" and thence "Ma'am" should the conversation continue.

## Roland's recommendation

**KEEP YOUR DISTANCE**

When a venue is being prepared to accept royalty there is always a very clear no-go zone, normally designated by the width of a red carpet. Never encroach on this area.

Imagine your chagrin if instead of greeting royalty you find yourself the centre of an extremely rushed but effective rugby scrum with you at its base and a plethora of security guards attempting to become intimate with your person!

# An anecdote

## Mind your Ps and Qs

It was indeed many years ago and our own beloved Royal Family were touring Australia.

During the tour, a tree felling competition was held in one of the more densely wooded areas of that great country, (not normally known for its forests). The competition was fast and furious; the lumberjacks were all vying to see who could impress Her Majesty the most.

In the hot sun of the summer afternoon the trees fell like nine pins and the sound of crashing wood could be heard throughout the vicinity. One by one the great trees fell, one by one the huge branches were lopped off, and one by one the felled branches were trimmed and piled up to show the completion of the task.

The winner was a particularly gigantic man who possessed, I feel sure, the ability to crack coconuts between his thumb and forefinger. The giant stood towering with his knuckles almost dragging on the ground as he was addressed by H.M. The Queen, "You must be an awfully strong fellow" she remarked. The reply came in the characteristic twang so renowned of the area, "Oh yes, Your Majesty. I could lift a f******g ton"! Amidst the gasps and the exclamations of horror H.R.H. The Duke of Edinburgh stepped forward pronouncing "I say, steady on". "Oh, alright then", acquiesced the fellow, "Half a f*****g ton"!

# The Season

"The Season" is the official name for that period in the calendar that normally lasts from Henley Royal Regatta until Queen Charlotte's Ball, when in the past all debutantes were presented at court. If you say the end of May until the beginning of September you won't be far off.

## Henley Regatta

Taking place at Henley-on-Thames this is the first of the official engagements of the social calendar. On each bank of the Thames there are two different types of party going on. On the Royal bank there is the serious matter of rowing and this is attended by members of the Royal family. On the opposite bank are the guests of large corporate organisations and other private parties.

Gentlemen wear blazers and flannels or cricket flannels. Ladies wear summer dresses or cocktail frocks. Very elegant. All this and strawberries too!

## The Royal Garden Party

It is perfectly possible you might receive an invitation to attend one of the series of garden parties held at Buckingham Palace and other establishments during the course of the season.

What does one wear? Over the years certain rules have been relaxed with regard to dress at Royal garden parties. At one time it was morning coat only, day dress for ladies. These days you might be informed to wear a simple lounge suit.

# The Queen's birthday parade

This spectacular event, The Trooping of the Colour, normally takes place on the 2nd Saturday in June and marks the official birthday of the monarch. It is held on Horse Guards Parade at Whitehall in London and it is possible you might one day receive an invitation to attend this.

And the dress code? For gentlemen it is dark lounge suit and a bowler hat if you have one. For ladies it is day dress and, of course, that wonderful hat you've been saving.

If you are serving in the military you will normally be expected to wear 'Blues' or their equivalent.

As Her Majesty the Queen arrives on Horse Guards Parade, you will be expected to stand and remove your hat, or salute if in uniform. Ladies must stand and bow slightly.

This is also done when the 'Colours' are paraded past you. The colours represent the regiment and all its honours.

# Balls to you!

Ah yes, the thrill of Wimbledon week. If you are attending, dress is quite informal unless you are attending the centre court and royalty is also destined to be there. You will be informed of any dress code. Normally the only stipulation is tie.

I warn you now, take your own strawberries. The price charged there is absolutely horrendous.

## Ascot week

One of the most glittering occasions in the calendar.
Anyone can attend and enjoy this magnificent royal race week.
The daily carriage procession from Windsor is one of the sights
of Britain.

Ascot Grey? Actually no! That which most people call Ascot
Grey is actually more properly Derby Grey. It is perfect for Derby
but for Ascot it should be black tailcoat, grey waist coat, grey
gloves, and striped trousers. This is all finished with a black silk
top hat.

If you pass any member of the Royal Family at the races you
raise your hat. This is only common courtesy.

And the ladies? Oh, my dear ladies! Now is the time for the
posh frock and the hat! Now is your time in the limelight.
Ascot is not Ascot without the perfectly stunning display
of formal day dresses and head turning hats.

But, don't forget to wear gloves. Think Audrey Hepburn, you
can't go wrong.

## Your knighthood

You never know, it could happen. If you are summoned to an
investiture the dress code for men is almost the same as that
for Ascot Week. A black tail coat, striped trousers with a black
waistcoat, grey gloves and a black silk top hat.

If kneeling for your knighthood, I beg you, no sudden
movements of the head. The sword is sharp. By the way,
did you know you also get a badge with it!

## Is the fat lady singing?

What about the opera? Great stuff, good music, and drinks at half time. Normally a dinner jacket for a man but ladies get to go overboard with evening dress. Something long and luscious.

The rules remain the same, if you are invited to meet a member of royalty then the bow and curtsey are unaltered. If you are in the body of the theatre then as soon as the Royal Party arrive in the Royal Box and the orchestra play the National Anthem, you stand and bow slightly towards the Royal Box.

## Roland's recommendation

**IT'S GONG TIME**

Wear medals when they are requested. If you're the only one you can feel like a total prune. This happened to me once, every one was resplendent in black tie and I was walking round looking like a mobile xylophone.

# Let us now recap on our expectations

- When your invitation arrives, read the instructions thoroughly.
- Comply with the dress code in every way.
- Keep your distance.
- Never, ever, reach out to touch or grab the Royal presence.
- Never offer your hand first.
- Speak in reply, don't make the first move.
- Remember it is "Ma'am" as in 'smarm'.
- Only wear medals when instructed to do so.
- Bow, or curtsey, with grace. Don't go too low.
- Remember 'Ascot Grey' is for Derby Day. For Ascot it is black tailcoat.
- Big hats ladies, but mind you don't 'take off'!
- Always gloves when meeting the Royal Family ladies.
- Blazers for Henley Regatta.
- Hats off for the dear old Queen.

# Ask the professor...

**Q** *Should you send thank you cards for Christmas or holiday gifts?*

**A** A thank you card should always be sent if you did not open the gift in the giver's presence.

**Q** *What is a polite way in which to turn down a dinner invitation, or indeed an invitation of any sort?*

**A** When you reply to an invitation and it is an occasion that you do not wish to attend or cannot attend, then merely respond by thanking the sender for their invitation but pointing out that unfortunately you have a previous engagement.

**Q** *What is the proper form of addressing a letter or card to a widow?*

**A** A recent widow may be addressed simply as Mrs. (her husband's name). However if she is not recently widowed as either Mrs. (her name) or Ms. (her name).

**Q** *In which direction should food be passed around the table?*

**A** Food should be passed to the right or anti-clockwise.

**Q** *Should you excuse yourself from the table if you wish to sneeze?*

**A** By all means excuse yourself, and never use your napkin as a handkerchief.

**Q** *Should a child stand or sit whilst adults are being seated at a table?*

**A** The child or children should stand behind their chair before all the adults are seated.

**Q** *If you have received a phone call from someone whose telephone number you did not have originally, but it was captured on caller ID, no message being left on your voicemail. Is it appropriate to call the person back?*

**A** No. It is appropriate to call someone back only when a person requests a call back and leaves their number voluntarily.

**Q** *Are speaker phones rude?*

**A** No simply ask permission before putting a person on your speaker phone. Be polite.

**Q** *What is the proper way to answer the telephone?*

**A** If at home it is customary to answer by quoting your telephone number. However when in the workplace it is more correct to answer with "hello" and then your name.

**Q** *What if someone is rude to you on the telephone?*

**A** Terminate the telephone call with a polite but subtle statement. For example "please excuse me, but I do not feel that this call should continue under these circumstances. Feel free to call me back when things are a little more settled. Thank you and goodbye!"

**Q** *Who should call back when disconnected on the telephone?*

**A** When there is poor telephone connection or when you are disconnected, the person that originated the call is responsible for calling back.

**Q** *What is the proper way to display good sportsmanship at a sporting event?*

**A** After playing any sport congratulate the other players, whether they have won or lost, letting them know you have enjoyed playing with them. Many professionals should take note of this.

**Q** *Where do I place my napkin when excusing myself from the table?*

**A** Place your napkin on your chair as it is totally inappropriate to put a soiled napkin on the table when others are still eating. At the end of the meal place your napkin to the left of your place sitting.

**Q** *How should we butter a slice of bread or a roll?*

**A** At the dining table the bread should always be broken in to pieces, then butter one small piece at a time.

# The last word...

It will be of interest to know, indeed some of you may remember, the mother of HRH the Duke of Edingburgh was HRH the Princess Andrew of Greece. Even though her christened name was Alice, upon the death of her husband she took on his name as his royal widow.

She was known as the princess Andrew of Greece until her demise.

Well dear reader, we have come to the end of our journey. As far as is possible I hope this little book will, to some extent, help you through the pitfalls and minefields of social etiquette.

It is impossible for me to express the debt of gratitude I owe to the many professional exponents of this great art with whom I have worked over many years.

In particular I must doff my hat in homage to the ladies and gentlemen who make up the personal staff to our Royal Family, and indeed their counterparts in all countries in the world. These doyens of all that is correct and proper rarely get the recognition that they deserve. Let me remedy that now.

Ladies and gentlemen, I salute you!

Roland

# Index

# 'The Greatest Tips in the World' books

*Baby & Toddler Tips*
by Vicky Burford
ISBN 978-1-905151-70-7

*Barbeque Tips*
by Raymond van Rijk
ISBN 978-1-905151-68-4

*Cat Tips* by Joe Inglis
ISBN 978-1-905151-66-0

*Cookery Tips*
by Peter Osborne
ISBN 978-1-905151-64-6

*Cricketing Tips*
by R. Rotherham & G. Clifford
ISBN 978-1-905151-18-9

*DIY Tips*
by Chris Jones & Brian Lee
ISBN 978-1-905151-62-2

*Dog Tips* by Joe Inglis
ISBN 978-1-905151-67-7

*Etiquette & Dining Tips*
by Prof. R. Rotherham
ISBN 978-1-905151-21-9

*Freelance Writing Tips*
by Linda Jones
ISBN 978-1-905151-17-2

*Gardening Tips*
by Steve Brookes
ISBN 978-1-905151-60-8

*Genealogy Tips*
by M. Vincent-Northam
ISBN 978-1-905151-72-1

*Golfing Tips*
by John Cook
ISBN 978-1-905151-63-9

*Horse & Pony Tips*
by Joanne Bednall
ISBN 978-1-905151-19-6

*Household Tips*
by Vicky Burford
ISBN 978-1-905151-61-5

*Personal Success Tips*
by Brian Larcher
ISBN 978-1-905151-71-4

*Podcasting Tips*
by Malcolm Boyden
ISBN 978-1-905151-75-2

*Property Developing Tips*
by F. Morgan & P Morgan
ISBN 978-1-905151-69-1

*Retirement Tips*
by Tony Rossiter
ISBN 978-1-905151-28-8

*Sex Tips*
by Julie Peasgood
ISBN 978-1-905151-74-5

*Travel Tips*
by Simon Worsfold
ISBN 978-1-905151-73-8

*Yoga Tips*
by D. Gellineau & D. Robson
ISBN 978-1-905151-65-3

## Pet Recipe books

*The Greatest Feline Feasts in the World* by Joe Inglis
ISBN 978-1-905151-50-9

*The Greatest Doggie Dinners in the World* by Joe Inglis
ISBN 978-1-905151-51-6

## 'The Greatest in the World' DVDs

*The Greatest in the World – Gardening Tips*
presented by Steve Brookes

*The Greatest in the World – Yoga Tips*
presented by David Gellineau and David Robson

*The Greatest in the World – Cat & Kitten Tips*
presented by Joe Inglis

*The Greatest in the World – Dog & Puppy Tips*
presented by Joe Inglis

For more information about currently available
and forthcoming book and DVD titles please visit:

# www.thegreatestintheworld.com

or write to:

**The Greatest in the World Ltd**
PO Box 3182
Stratford-upon-Avon
Warwickshire CV37 7XW
United Kingdom

Tel / Fax: +44(0)1789 299616
Email: info@thegreatestintheworld.com

# The author

Professor, Doctor, Roland Rotherham has enjoyed a varied and exciting life ranging from serving on the personal staff of Her Majesty Queen Elizabeth II and travelling with Her Majesty to many countries in the world, assisting in the organising of state occasions and private functions for some of the world's elite, to becoming a world renowned authority on King Arthur and the Holy Grail, lecturing internationally on this subject to ever growing audiences.

His advice is constantly sought on 'how to do it right' and invitations to dinner or drinks at his home (affectionately known as Roly Towers) are jealously sought after.

Professor Rotherham lives alone in Staffordshire in what he describes as 'faded elegance'; he relaxes with his books, entertaining and his beloved cricket.